SWALLOWING THE SCROLL

Late in a Prophetic Tradition
with the Poetry
of Susan Howe and John Taggart

LEW DALY

———

apex of the M *supplement #1*
Buffalo, New York

The author would like to thank Pam Rehm, Alan Gilbert, Kristin Prevallet, and especially Robert Creeley and Dennis Tedlock for their support.

frontispiece: reproduction of an untitled engraving from Jacob Böhme's *Mysterium Magnum*

back-cover epigraph from Abiezer Coppe's *Some Sweet Sips of some Spirituall Wine* (1649)

M Press
P.O. Box 247
Buffalo NY 14213-0247

ISBN 1-879645-08-4

Fear, and the pit, and the snare, *are* upon thee, O inhabitant of the earth.

And it shall come to pass, *that* he who fleeth from the noise of the fear shall fall into the pit; and he that cometh up out of the midst of the pit shall be taken in the snare: the windows from on high are open, and the foundations of the earth do shake.

—Isaiah (24:17-18)

Now I intreat this and no more favour, that when God shall open my mouth, you that intend to persecute when my words are speaking, bid me deliver that state in writing unto you, and I will do it; for what I shall declare, I will give it under my hand, and also maintain it.

—Thomas Tany (a.k.a. THEAURAUIOHN
High Priest to the IEWES, 1654)

CONTENTS

Having taken into account certain of the most explicit demands of context in their work, I could not continue to write within the limits of what began here as a more formal review of recent publications by the poets Susan Howe and John Taggart; the type of articulation to which I was initially reconciled did not accommodate what had inspired me to speak. Yet beyond even the demands of context as well, this review has been transformed, if only overtaken, by a polemic that is itself falling prey to a terrible dream, relished only with tears, but brought to bear against the profane for many days. A petition brought to bellowing by apologetics, repetition, the diremptions of this wretched age, cannot, of course, in all modesty, situate itself as such except by way of pathos or some other less identifiable extreme. I take, then, as a model for the immodesty of my claims for them, the immodesty of the poems themselves—but considered as nakedness, and as having come before God out of fear and not credence or need. What I've made of their work may be properly understood—in the broadest sense of our efforts as those who must speak—as a call for reformation. Without, I'll admit, adequate qualification, I have come to take for granted the proximity to one another that their work continuously intimates, a proximity that, in person, they themselves acknowledge as abiding. Rhetorical justification of this—of what at times borders on being a hermeneutic conflation of the work of two ostensibly, or formally, so different poets—has been subordinated to a broader sense of the efforts of their poetries within an Anglo-American prophetic tradition of the written word. My effort, in turn, is one of a redoubling of the urgency in their work; I take as my method what might in part be characterized as an instigation of the lexicons at hand. Let me begin by saying, then, that no denial of revelation—of an access of the sacred to a page, or of divinity in the tip of a tongue to the structures of gain—can continue to be supported by a monumentalization of language in the face of that which it is unable to shadow, which shatters all systematicity and gain with the face of God: with the lineal and the illegible as givens of the page, but at a level, then, beyond all conceivable dichotomy of content and form, and beyond all *priority* of form, the revelatory is addressed and given access to these poems. To respond to these poems on their own terms, however, is not to simply see to it that revelation is received, but to prepare ourselves to see that it does not desist.

In the first instance it must be admitted that both poets have a share, and have to some extent created, or portended to our poetry this share in what among the young will come to pass as an irreconcilable but revitalizing rift, perhaps one among many, within the avant-garde—within and yet, if time permits, in a reality beyond the arts. To the degree to which it will contribute to the categorical, as opposed to the self-authorized, uprooting of the avant-garde, the virtue of this passionate rift within hypocrisy, between Enlightenment and non-Enlightenment conceptions of material and dissent, must be proclaimed. We will write with the ardor of a lower life-form, reserving for exteriority the higher. We are daily brought to bear against the profane by a face in the square, by a hand in the gears. Others have called fideistic what in Taggart's work is visionary, and what is antinomian in the work of Howe. But there can be no doubt that, notwithstanding the more monolithic and debilitating problem of the university-entrenched poetics of emotion and expression in the mainstream, forced reflection in the arts as well, remorselessly taking hold as it has by evading approach in the panopticon of non-absorption and prioritized form— and having reached its peak ingeniously, utopian in its reasoning but not its reach—must be relinquished if we wish, as well we must, to be dragged down, having brought to bear as we have the very dearth to which our lips must now be pressed, the very dearth from which our words must raise a furor first, and for the wicked make from dearth a furious grave of words. What we lack is a desire to subordinate, rather than render irreconcilable, what we know to what cannot be known—to what might welcome us if we corrupt the self, in ecstasy, and curse the words securing victory for the core; but what we lack is not subordinate to the word. Text-centricity disbands address, and yet essentializes lack. Burdened on all sides by compromise and nominalism, we will wager in a drastic shift—left nameless for now—a language in direct contrast to textualization. If there is nothing outside the text, then dissolution must be our counterhistory. We relish a collapse in the long-since problematically internalized hegemony of "innovation"—which is always a privilege—as the marker of radical ideology in the arts; in the interest of a world the not yet literal, but far more profitable death of which is what is necessarily wagered in a writing of autonomy and predeterminacy into texts, perhaps we must admit, concerning poetry, that what only *appears* to transform discloses *only* another hegemony. Many serious poets at work today have limited themselves to the idea that, having rid themselves of the conventionality intrinsic to their backgrounds as members of the upper classes, what lies ahead may only be approached through, or accommodated by, the power of innovation—of self-conscious unconventionality. Yet distinctions, not necessarily dichotomous, must be made—especially here in terms of what sets the work of both Howe and Taggart apart from the rest of the radical poetry of their generation between the unconventional and the heteronomous, between reflection and absolution, between irony and paradox, difference and non-indifference, the liminal and the limitless, etc. These are in fact wildly religious poetries, as profoundly anomalous as they are traditional, as irreverent as they are devotional, as resolutely at odds with current trends in the avant-garde as they are with those in the mainstream as well.

I mean to address the achievements of these two poets specifically in regard to two recent publications: Howe's *The Nonconformist's Memorial* and Taggart's *Loop*. Not at this time being capable of addressing these collections in full, I have chosen to focus my comments on a single poem in each; the poems I have chosen ("The Nonconformist's Memorial" and "The Rothko Chapel Poem"), however, are demonstrative of what most interests me in the work of these two poets in general, and in keeping with what they share as far as "poetics" goes, that being a radical regard for spirit and prophecy. I will provisionally describe by the word "prophecy" here a poetry that might be said to permit—on a stage of public hierarchy, and under the full weight of our disgrace as citizens on such a stage—enunciation in an encounter with the supra-hierarchical, the power of God. Leaving aside any endemic ignorance of their sources, pervasive as this ignorance may be at this time, however, we should instruct ourselves in an awareness of the work of these poets not simply at the level of the "religious," but more specifically, or rather, more historically in terms of an Anglo-American radical Protestant tradition. Indeed the work of Howe and Taggart may rightly be said to occupy, in different ways, but for similar reasons, the precarious place of poetry in a radical Protestant tradition, or, more generally, in a prophetic tradition of the written word.[1] In the early Protestantism of the kind to which these poems may be ascribed originated the very possibility of modern counterhistory. We have here

[1] I would emphasize, as well, that my use of the word "prophetic" is not meant to stand in opposition to a use of the word "mysticism." While the Western mystical traditions—and there *are* continuities between Jewish and Christian mysticism, effaced as they may be by the merely religious distinctions between them—do, on the whole, preclude prophecy, the prophetic tradition actually presupposes mysticism. To the extent to which mysticism is fixed in an itinerary of salvation, and not in a pursuit of the millenium, the prophetic is habitually forgone by mystics. But to the extent to which God-given justification has been continually compromised by clerical and magisterial mediation, mysticism, as a language of immediacy between the believer and God, came to be implicit to the prophetic turn in Reformation religio-political discourse. The complex history of the mystical lineage of the Reformation—in Eckhart, Tauler, *Eine Deutsche Theologie*, etc.—is fascinating, and of great interest in terms of the complexities involved in an attempt to understand the poetries of Howe and Taggart in terms of religion. While I nominate this work specifically to a Protestant prophetic tradition, I am by no means unaware of, or uninterested in, other "traditions" to which this work is at times indebted: e.g. a Marian tradition in Howe's "The Nonconformist's Memorial," or a medieval mystical tradition in the work of Taggart.

in our midst among the last and most radical intimations of this possibility. Their participation in the Protestant tradition must be understood in terms of the historical, though much overshadowed role of the vernacular Bible—especially the Prophets and the Apocalypse—in peasant revolts, in conventicle-style and prophetic feminism, in mystical anti-clericalism, in proto-communism and messianic anarchism, in black emancipation; but in terms of the poetries themselves we must understand this mutual interest in the Bible less at the expense of an emphasis placed on their differences, in terms of form, than at the expense of careless observation, either of the role of sacred power in the work—figured as that of the God of Exodus, Ezekiel, Mary or John—or of the work as a continuum of such power, conceived as spirit in the antinomian tradition. Sometimes not even with good intentions, those readers who have shown an interest, especially in the work of Howe—Taggart's work being perhaps even less assimilable—have demonstrated little more than an incidental recognition of, and often complete, even willful ignorance of many, if not most, of the historical, historiographical, theological, and mystical resources to which this work is beholden and from which it is and always has been drawn. Though I can barely begin to focus on the most prominent of these sources—the Authorized Version—I can offer in advance of future rectitude the thought that we must continuously begin to bring to life what gets lost through, and to speak to what is silenced by, appropriation of any kind. Reinscribed as avant-garde, to be a heart cut-out and made the variable, and not the iconoclasm, of a body of seditions from which the poem—thus severed by discourse— is therefore relativized out of range and bathed in light, the work of Howe and, even more marginally, that of Taggart, lives on inimitably in our minds, and as it is intended to live: as material testimony to an encounter with the heteronomous, or to encounter as such, in terms of what is in the first instance a criteriology of the divine. Howe and Taggart are, perhaps invariably, in fact pneumatic poets late in an Anglo-American prophetic tradition stretching from Wycliffe to Melville and Dickinson, but not beyond them, in full, until now. Yet similarly to the way in which the religiosity of an abolitionist such as Garrison, of emancipators such as Toussaint and King, of messianic/mystic anti-capitalists such as Benjamin, Bloch and Weil, is finally, but not least of all, a politics of the name: the poets in one way or another refuse to assign to iniquity anything less than absolute status—the status of a signature—in the historical process, and anything less than continuous resistance in the process of counterhistory. Milton assigned the mediators to perdition in the conclusion to *Of Reformation*. Now we are trying to assign meaning to the struggle against mediators. Poetry is both a consequence and herald of this express, if not now recognized defeat. *In extremis* then, we must ask what any consequence of writing at an angle to—but in despair of, not capitulation to—victorious textuality and death, might now require of us where corpses too are virtualized, and reinscribed, as signs of structure not of flesh; let there be fire in our eyes and loss of face when we begin to speak.

DEUS ABSCONDITUS

[I am] forced to proceed like the materialist—that is, by observation and experience—and to conclude in the language of the believer, because there is no other.

—Pierre Proudhon (from *System of Economical Contradictions*, 1846, trans. 1888)

Having come out of exile into a ceremony only of concord in the death-toll and the billfold . . . having first been revealed out of fire, to be immured within the heart but not inscribed by fire, the word of God perforce historicized in sound brought down the heavens to the entrance of Elijah's cave. Having come as a voice out of exile to make the flesh expound, of a sudden all utterance on the earth is to come from the one who must weep. From out of nothing having come as the sensorium of an historical God, and having been impugned until the relished time of parricide arrives too late to not interpolate a thralldom far more vast than that which worlds endure—a second exodus from which the hierarchs cannot withdraw—the *alarum* of our utterance continues on, resisting as it does all poetry but that which calls. Let us take ourselves out of this picture, and into the grand iconomachia of such a call.

Gloriously to no uncertain degree do we speak in being attuned to a renewal of attenuated debts, erupting only in the manner of our indebtedness to what is beyond all reconciliation with human indifference. Glorious only in its discontent, to dis-attenuate this historicity from which the living, like the dead, themselves refrain or are otherwise kept—so an utterance too, in the poem not unlike on the wing in a bind, but diachronic like the recondite stroke of a clock soaked in blood, becomes portentous in these times of which our world is not the vanguard but the part at large, or even more, bestirs a faultline in the finitude behind which fires roar. The utterance steeps in amnesty a writing of these times that is itself at war. Thus running the risk of being led headlong and having to exalt an abyss: one who has the ears to hear a message must say *come*.

On the pages and in images before the eyes of those empowered over poetry, who have with such insipience and antipathy so consistently restored it all to the status of aesthetic artifact—the very *in absentia* of historicity—steps must be taken to reclaim from them the poem as a sensorium for the call. Based nearly endlessly in ashes if not filled with them to the core, atop a pyre or in the line of fire, the page must thus address and as a once more millenial harbinger effect redemption in the diction of a remnant at war and yet worshipping love. Now we must permit of no response that is not in itself an exposure to the spiritual force of our duty to those who will call. Other than the decision of utterance itself—the exposure already enough to uphold such a call— almost nothing atones for our violence now. A language not least of all formless, but overexposed, says it all. All that's the lot, not the soul, of a language in chains may be proferred by us, or be offered to those who will call, through our use of it now. What cannot but be heard coming out from within any mouth—that which we nevertheless cannot yet name— is a call.

Inspired in terms of and in witness to the presence of a call, indeed our part in it now radicalized as a universality only of ruins is necessarily without end, but of consequence as a prophecy of the wind. In what way either in or out—in conflagration or annihilatory doubt—may it be known that we must heed it now? What is a word for the word? The transcendental signified does not exist. Thus the name of God is not a signifier of transcendence, because there is a God. God is the signifier of all that existence transcends. Ours is, as never before, an endeavor of the transcended, religion in an existence the loss of which cannot itself be suppressed. Not as a sound-image, but as a giver of signs is God the "signifier," the "that which signifies," of which I speak. But I am speaking of love under another name. Only in a manner of speaking do the living have an inner sanctum. The inner sanctum is asymmetry. The moment at which we speak must never cease.

Does the question of how one might turn the tables on the dialectic ring true? At all costs including those of the decalogue and the dialectic, perhaps our model of community must be Masada. In the theodicy we've seen, the mobs at obelisks are each a God; to the extent to which the violence reveals a voice, the crowd, be it brought to its knees or not,   is heteronomous, and must be crowned. We will be trying to admit of a sublimity to the general strike—in a manner of speaking: semioclasm ministering unto the status quo a blow from within the without, being ministered to the point of immediacy by a people's claims.

Why there are no longer any faces in the crowd of, say, the "moral economy" of E.P. Thompson's artisan/ grain-rioters, may have less to do with differences between early and late anti-capitalism than it has to do with differences between the early and late versions of labor in the history of industrial capitalism. Yet one can hardly grasp the scale of our failure at the level of community except in terms of a capitulation—en masse—to the modern and the myth of progress at the level of media and machines. Simone Weil was once at pains to point out that "what a country calls its vital economic interests are not the things which enable its citizens to live, but the things which enable it to make war; petrol is much more likely than wheat to be a cause of international conflict." The extent to which our compliance, with the wishes endemic to this myth and to its ravages, has overcome all possibility of community can hardly be overestimated. The critique of antimodernism as nostalgic is itself far more nostalgic—for the time when the *modern*, not the *virtual*, was inescapable—than the Luddite is. Technologically speaking, then, only history is without end—not because a history driven by changes in technology is non-teleological, but because it has yet to begin; future generations of revolutionaries, that is, will have as their goal the historicization of technology, which will ensue, of course, if only from the point at which technology meets its end. One needn't be, as I am not, a rational Marxist critic of the free-market, or a sophisticated critic of Marxism, to despise as oxymoronic the notion of a revolutionary technology. In fact, with Foucault who, more by implication of a different methodology than because of ideological differences, rejected an exclusively class-based critique of power, we can go so far as to include certain "advances in medicine" among the more deceptive oxymorons constituting the controlling modern myth of progress, hegemonically bound up as these changes in treatment are in a humanist political agenda that, for the right, harbors at best only a certain appeal to, at worst a call to arms over, the "quality of life." But might we not permit ourselves a moment of non-reflection during which we resist the dialectic as reductive but nevertheless reduce to a call for neo-Luddism the entirety of anti-capitalist strategy since the late 18th century?

Steps must be taken at this time as if they scarcely separate inexhaustible finitude from the infinite understood as a lack of ground. Poetry restores in us that desire to destroy any order of things *which does not supercede our capacity to oppose ourselves to things taken as objects opposed to a subject*. For in language we are always approaching this moment at which, even as it moves toward dissolution, "being" is likely to ebb as though in having found an outpost, of flows from nothing if not from the material force of love. In freeing the other from form the poem must incline us toward a course of substitution less with its origin in God, than heteronomous without a source—but more historical than not, as a sensorium for the call. How often mocked and banished have the prophets been, who have thus predisposed the poem to infiltration from a word of overlorded force—from out of the depths a word conformed or from the moment of reform a word imposed—or in the latter days if not yet now, who have it all held-forth as advent set in stark relief against a backdrop of the possibility, which is the historicity, of such a word. The revelation from beyond but on the tongue may give way and yet take what it will; but by breathing us past every word, and by never leaving the world as words pass us along the messiah arrives at all times. Doomed by words to be wanderers on a skyline severed from the heavens and the land; heteronomously called, like water-bearers caught on a whalebrow overhanging the flow of, then the whole of time; renounced as subhuman, at large under the charge of a destruction no longer preemptory to, but definitively following upon our godliness as a throng; gathered, brought low "at the prow," and yet casting for our fare in this flow as it ushers us in: we must prepare for what, when here, will not have always been, for what, indeed, there will be left to give, that we may come to this outpost of the ebb and flow of our punishment over time, where beckoning is itself the last command, saying that it may seek another of its avatars or at last recede under fire from the destroyers of language and then a voice alone.

Mystic insurrectionaries have said that we must not concede, but that we will do so clinging to shards of a circle of sign and significance that we must first of all trample under our feet, but then embrace to provide a space in which the shards may lodge. At the ends of all shards such as these we as lovers must remain impaled and speak. In doing so a polity no less at risk than individual life will develop as if around anarchy—the gap of God—and thus relinquish space so as not to avoid the possibility of wanton embrace. Shards of the law now ground-down to and convergent in a single point, or, the tip of a shard in the heart heteronomously dislodged, and impolitic all too idolatrously to the point (of bringing annihilation upon itself), must now be offered-up before enormous crowds. What but ruination brought to our impunity will flush us out from under shelter of the law? By what, that is, will we be brought if only logically beyond the end of, or else to bear without a parallel to, election in an arbitrary line? Of our debts to that which is irreconcilable with human indifference, an amassment now no longer at bay but quite literally wanton among us must form from all manner of utterance a sign of the offering of signs. Like shafts of light bearing images of a vision of history to the prisoner's eye, the line is a sign of the offering of signs. This is the feat of the line—that it may put out our eyes like a needle the fiery eye of which is itself put out by ecstasy, in waves: a needle not to widen our eyes in its passing inside us, but, in igniting us by passing us by, to have widened whatever horizons inhibit desire and unite only signs. For it is by virtue of the very means by which we must nevertheless proclaim it that the truth escapes. If only endlessly or in ecstasy, then, and if not otherwise overcome: at the moment of which we may proclaim no truths, the means by which such moments come to pass blaze a path to God. We have faces not otherwise seen, and yet not, if not hidden from God, ever free from reproach, or from form or from being alone, for more than a moment in any given dialogue or poem. Only to that which has yet, as a voice, to fall silent or be heard as a force, may we offer ourselves in response to a call. We are hearing a call coming forth from a thicket of forms; flame from the thicket that gave to Moses the name of God has come across the centuries and from hearth to hearth, themselves engulfed in this process by eternal flames.

There is nothing more for which we must fail to wait except exteriority: our task is to usher it in. Once the flesh around a bullet the penetration of which is without end, swallows by analogy the phallus of the assassin and centers our rage, sentences hitherto handed down by us now destine us to fulfill a judgment that we cannot make—as though in preparation for our coming to face, and be disgraced by, what we've made. I am saying that a dialogue moors in our eyes as the orbit of God, and our voice as a face-to-face people, though born under fire, rises up and is suddenly a cry, then a throng. Clinging to the shards which cannot be dislodged, we must get caught in the trappings of a move-ment of signification on-route toward hidden stores of a vigilance formerly frenzied but never espied, yet bordering quite literally on dissolution as uninhibitable solicitude, the antithesis to war. We must each in our own way refuse to keep pace with the autonomy of words, by reigning-in and letting-out the heat beneath, and letting sparks descend upon the line-length-like tinder of language loosed as if to quite literally lodge an incessant attention to it in each-other's eyes as dwindling, then rekindled flame—an attention working in tandem with, but against us in time, tending as time does to play with fire when we look away. Moving entireties be-tween opposites, and opposites through fire, then, the line is like the edge of the wild—a path well-travelled yet unworn, if always only in folly like theodicy, martyrdom, ritual and war.

A poetry unable to cast shadows because the light that strikes it comes from within itself is like a face; just as the face in a crowd can only *re*-appear, poetry intervenes in the anonymity of language, in the effacement of meaning within the regime of capital, but without projecting onto pages even a silhouette of its destiny as an eschaton for our rage. A poem may be said to have risen off the page when it affects the reader's face. And yet a face not yet seen is changed immediately to glare and takes command, that we ourselves may be revealed by what we cannot bear to see. Destruction wreathes us in around this countenance in which our image, there reflected and enraged, cannot be read. "What could have been" is what this image actually is.

Indeed immediacy is required of that through which none of us here have yet ceaselessly lived. Poetry too comes only in the wake of a withdrawal of that from which we ourselves are not permitted to withdraw. We must therefore make a point of maintaining as a divergence in kind and not degree the distinction between a process and a departure. We must take only the most disallowable of our burdens, not just into account, but quite literally upon ourselves in being called out. Neither blind nor lame itself, a community of substitution and a scream, of the lame transported on the shoulders of the blind they guide, is the object of all poeisis thus redefined as an attempt to stay alive by becoming enraged. The wandering cause of the other within, yet resisting, the same, is not in any sense a sign. Perhaps the movement of meaning in a community kept from loosing it through the use of words nevertheless signifies a trace not yet completely abandoned either *by* the divine, or *to* the system of signs: we are bound to one another as signs of the offering of signs. In poetry the burden of our having been unburdened of the requirements of others by the impossibility of community must become too much. The denial of prophetic rectitude, the impossibility, not of founding a community, but of being founded on the basis of it, ruinously to all but love, is the basis upon which our blindness to others at this time is the final superstructure, the site of uncontested anonymity.

Wittgenstein's later thinking provides us with one among a number of powerful antidotes to the foundational desire for a transcendental, or rather, for an independent or objective basis of signification, but perhaps the "systematic," or, if totalized, the "constitutive" functioning of language is itself simply the most ironic *symptom* of, rather than an analytic *alternative* to, a violence more thoroughly prohibitive of desire and the outside than any instrumentalization or absorption is. As Levinas, to the philosophical community, found it necessary to say of Nietzsche's amoralismn thirty years ago, perhaps we might cautiously say that the Wittgensteinian inquiry into (turned paradigm of) the limits and powers of language is in no sense except the historical of the same import to us as it was (and still is) to the radical poets who came of age during the post-JFK era of American supremacy. The limits/powers of language determine themselves only in terms of, not *as* terms of, what is made available for circulation at the level of meaning by the authorities over a given cultural moment—in our time the media moguls. Of course implicit in such an understanding of language is an acute awareness of the fact that the historical process is at this stage a complete conspiracy. As a professional philosopher Wittgenstein was of course unaware of the *extent* to which, in even the most practical or dynamic sense, language as such does not simply "exist": that which is, as language, now in use is in the first instance always piped-in from the superstructure. What to Wittgenstein was an object of practical inquiry and situational analysis is itself subject to violent manipulation— not, that is, as a quasi-empirical, quasi-constitutive medium of semantic exchange, but as an ideologically accommodating medium of conspiratorial cultural production. If only for reasons of what is now its "a-culturality," then, the thinking of Wittgenstein too, as opposed to that of his Viennese contemporary Karl Kraus, in *Die Fackel*, must be considered an artifact of the analytic tradition, and therefore understood—without undue irony in light of its pragmatic methodology—as a rarefication, a depoliticization of language. Is it naive, moreover, to think preposterous the entire proposition of an English-language avant-garde poetry informed largely, if only implicitly, by Russian and European structuralist linguistics, considering the fact that this imported discourse has been appropriated on the basis of English translations of texts written in, and therefore about, languages with different structures than that of English? But more importantly, the question must be raised as to whether or not linguistics as a discipline is of any relevance for the possibility of poeisis in a world in which "language itself," even as pragmatically as Wittgenstein understood it, does not exist in our communities independently of market-driven codification and subliminality.

As poets we are thus left with a choice between, on the one hand, a reflective mimesis of the virtuality and atomization of language in an information age, and, on the other, an appeal to the non-linguistic as a provenance for redemption from all thralldoms other than those of the lover to his or her heart, or those of the prophet, or mystic, to his or her demon or god. For the time being let us accord to this distinction the status of a Manichaean dualism. I have tried to find meaning, again, in a theological idea of language as influx, but leading to love in the most public sense—that of apocalpyse—attributable to such a word. To reinvent a theological idea of language I have attempted to look—here and elsewhere—at the figural, the typological, the locutionary and the rhetorical methods, and at the political and historical presuppositions, by virtue of which texts in a prophetic tradition attempt to situate themselves, either *as* the word of God, or in unique relation to the possibility of such a word. And in the writings of d'Olivet, Walter Benjamin and Karl Kraus, and Michel de Certeau, I have sought not for a theory of language, but for an afterword to all reflection: not, that is, for an Adamic language per se, but for a language of the nonlinguistic—of the heteronomous in any utterance that can direct us toward the extreme demands that radical meaning, the revelatory and the counterhistorical in poetry, places on the very possibility, always structuralist, of a conception of "language itself," independent of offering, of egress and influx, excess and reception.

Michel de Certeau's marginality as a historian, as opposed to his prominence as a theorist, goes hand in hand with his centralization of mystic speech as a, if not *the*, most radically historical, because unrealizable, discourse of the Renaissance: "The endlessness of instants that are beginnings create, therefore, a historicity in which continuities lose their pertinence, just as institutions do." Even now we must begin to understand by the word "structure," then, not simply that which, at the level of syntax, systemicizes language, but that which, within a range of transparencies from the conventional to the mystical, denies exteriority its instrument by censoring asymmetrical address. Let us not overlook, moreover, the extent to which a language may, in effect, remain uninhabited by the gestures presupposing it. It is indeed to this very extent that an ethical resistance to language is in turn further radicalized by—which is to say further subordinated to—an exteriority the only movement of which is actually made by the significations it provokes and conforms. Such gestures at that which is signified, if only as imminence, do not merely direct us toward what cannot be reached in language—though they do this also—but they actually make of their own dependence on language a vestige from which we are swept away by them. Thus being tantamount to what some have experienced as ecstasy, others as anarchy, a poetry perceived as being left in the wake of, but as a premise of, a gesture in this way can actually vestigialize the assimilations—for example of the law—by virtue of which our debt to the inordinate, or rather, our subordination to alterity, has always lapsed. A gesture that is in the last instance still a premise of the language, and even the poem, in which it is represented necessarily shatters opacity, but is itself outshone by light on the absurd. But an idea of God in all opacity of, which is the systematicity of, what is given and withheld within our use of words, is patterned after recesses of the absurd as such—recesses the missing link of which is the prophetic word. Such is, of course, the status of all paradox as well; the unspeakable may exist at the level of, but not, in all instances, necessarily *within* the language in the manner of which it extends itself to one who speaks.

However transparent, the paradoxicality of even a gesture of radical displacement to the outside of language cannot in any but the most theoretical sense be completely contained; all paradox as such is necessarily exposed by what is blinding us, and always in pronounced defiance of the frame within which the difference produced through a mirroring of language comes to glimmer as currency in a volatile, but closed exchange. Empires, on the other hand, are being based on the play of signifiers; the least vulnerable, because most sublimated, of these empires is that of academic theory. The persuasions of deferment, like those of leeching during the plague years, are wearing thin under the weight of an amassment of physical pain; a millenium already lost to our deferment to the one we've left behind will necessarily tend toward only the most profane of cataclysms. The "play" of signifiers is a far more rigid and exclusionary process—a dogma really—than it appears to be, to the degree to which the distinction between a process and a departure is foreclosed by play. Let us take to heart the image of Odysseus evading the Sirens as an emblem for the contemporary avant-garde. What appears, in their work, to be shattered, is also intrinsic—a mirroring; what is denied as transparent provokes an explosion. Limited as it is, then, to the formal effects of the presumption that transparency is wanting in (critical) footholds for the possibility of social consciousness, the "play" of signifiers is in fact not just—or not at all—a praxis for radical, or transformative, critiques of transparency, but rather it is a language of the very hegemony of critique itself, at what is clearly and intentionally the end of this all too brief literary-historical process by which poetry, as opposed to university press free-verse, has come to face not just its own extinction, though not the extinction facing the world either; we shall not countenance the extinction of the very modes of address—such as prophecy, praise, petition, lament, admonition, litany, exhortation, testimony, etc.—of which poetry is the common denominator, and the only repository as well. Shestov said that many turning-points in, and sources of, the history of Western thought have been a consequence of the struggle of philosophers to fend-off renewed efforts on the part of biblical thinkers to change the *and* between "Athens and Jerusalem" to an *or*. Like Protagoras who "glorified the arbitrary," Heraclitus, Isaiah, and St. Paul may be said to stand, together within the dialectic of Socratic knowledge and the unknowable, on the side of the unknowable against which Socrates took his stand wearing the mask of virtue. Among the most basic and disastrous patronages of the great epistemological periplum for which Western history has been the tortured pack-mule must be counted, first and foremost, our refusal to deny to the death of Socrates all consideration as a martyrdom.

How, then, do we rather attempt to refrain from keeping silent than continue to deny that we are unwilling—not unable—to listen when another speaks? Why are we unable—not unwilling—to refrain from manifesting terror in each other's eyes? Might we be so bold as to offer, however, to those who have called, a language against the systematicity of which the very moment that we enter into it—the very moment at which we must utter it—harbors only a challenge, from the standpoint not of a reflective acceptance of difference, but of ecstatic non-indifference in responsibility? Upon reflection we always find that an aversion to obligations more finite, or of a finitude even more inexhaustible than that which a concept of "difference" permits, is like a roll of the dice. With any luck we end up owing nothing to, or feeling nothing but a freedom from being interminably obliged by, the other before our eyes, perceived until now as an image of God, but now deified in an asymmetry the disproportionateness of which is unparalleled even by the passion of Christ. We feel a horror that unites our lies even as it is relieved by them, and even if we remain silent or foreground the signs. Pain cannot as such be read; the mandate of textualization is painless, and must therefore stand accused of being an instrument of pain. For those who live rather than see through it, the textuality of any given moment of time is the very threshold of pain.

Like Melville among the crypto-positivists of his time, many of us are finding that we have been forced, by a certain priority of the role of non-indifference over that of difference, toward a radical, rather than general, skepticism. We are skeptical not just of the possibility of knowledge, presence, communication, etc., but of the possibility of skepticism as well. Skepticism must leave us defenseless, not unaccountable. Felled as we one day must be by a call to which language as we know it has deafened us, the time has now come for us to admit of no questions other than those for which the answers do not so much exist or not exist, as come continuously to pass upon demand, but not to bear until the end, in repetition, is more literally at hand. A questioning of questioning necessarily sets skepticism, having sacrificed the power of knowledge to itself, on its head insofar as power itself, beyond the contingencies endemic to its operating at the level of knowledge, is painstakingly acquired by the only seemingly unretentive skeptic. But the radical skeptic is buffeted back with great force by a struggle into which the very tenets of our exoneration from conventionality have prevented us from entering without delay. I am speaking of the struggle against iniquity. The paradox of our confrontation with a questioning that is itself called unanswerably into question is necessarily self-annihilatory to the extent to which the questioner harbors no irony toward the unanswerable. Whereas irony as we know it is to some extent a consequence of the skepticism for which modern science, and its counterpart—the ravages of technocracy—are responsible, paradox is without consequence except at the level of sacrifice. Having lost, that is, the advantage of questioning to the non-oppositional demands of the unanswerable, the radical skeptic is left without the power of both belief *and* disbelief, being torn as such to pieces of it all. Let us thus admit that Hawthorne is to this day the best reader of Melville.

Opened only to the contra-identical, the non-dialectical, the supra-hierarchical, having lost the power of belief and disbelief, we have found in ourselves a sudden synchrony with what is nothing other than—and never more utterly so than now—the lack of time. Our questioning of skepticism does not, as it does so well for the positivist, obtain to a return to knowledge via a different route—in this case that of the unquestionable or structural—but rather it gets put to us heteronomously, in dispensations not of sublimity and immanence, but of groundlessness and immediacy, and in league not with atheism but parricide. Now is thus the moment for us to effect, in this most radical sense of our efforts as those who must speak, the decision of prophecy. We must move beyond both the conflation of, and the dichotomy of, content and form, into a morass comprised of each day more impassable but revolutionary paths between irony and act, between material availability and uninhibited love. This movement renders viable what must at all costs be understood as the first moment of time to disclose irreversible anarchy. Just as a type of momentarily incarnate nothingness at once makes way for and proceeds from a summit formed from organs during the act of love, in the same motion the drives of the world, now at large, move us closer to a cry requiring depths not within but among us, and requiring no uncertain loss of control if even just an echo over the roar of nothingness is to be heard from our voices below.

The rhetorical question to which the very fact of our speaking in language is itself the only answer necessarily takes hold of us in a manner of speaking conditioned by the mystery of God. We must search for the rhetorical question to which the very fact of our speaking at all is itself the only answer and for which it is the only known condition. In this search the answer will not satisfy the questioner unless we ourselves refuse to raise the question put to us in the presence of words. Conceding space to influx and the other's face in what is nevertheless, no less than excess itself, unintentional in the dominion of love, we must not, however, permit ourselves to taste of the impunity we will deny to the annihilators of love. Only those poets who refuse the heteronomous yoke of the neighbor and God—and both require our attention to labor under the same yoke—will succeed. But the failure of those who labor under this yoke will be the only love. Prophecy uncircumscribed by the orifices of a mask through which all words received must be poured, can by necessity only be undertaken in the presence of a spark, but at a climax continuously toward which we are brought by the power of God. We must permit ourselves the liberty of calling forth from history another, far less ordered course: only the inalienableness of ownership will suffer literally from a continuous attenuation at the end.

Over the glory of what point or manner of access to us has the mask through which prophecy strikes come to rest? The either/or of heteronomy is not a binary, but a divide. Levinas says that language is itself prophecy, and that, if figured, prophecy must not on any account fail to grant meaning to all of our acts as though a transference of bread from one's own mouth into the mouth of the unfed other were the prototype of every word we speak. For Simone Weil the abyss of revelation was the space of her experience with the point of a nail the head of which is the entire universe between the individual and God; she experienced the revelation as a hammerblow transposed from crucifixion to her senses during work and prayer. A sense of affliction under another name overcame her desire to live through the Second World War.

THE BOWER AND THE ABYSS

No man saw awe, nor to his house
Admitted he a man
Though by his awful residence
Has human nature been.

Not deeming of his dread abode
Till laboring to flee
A grasp on comprehension laid
Detained vitality.

Returning is a different route
The Spirit could not show
For breathing is the only work
To be enacted now.

"Am not consumed," old Moses wrote,
"Yet saw him face to face"—
That very physiognomy
I am convinced was this.

—Emily Dickinson

The Gospel According to Mary

> This is the *woman* that compasseth a man;
> who comprehend God manifest in their
> flesh, who carry forth the glorious
> discoveries of the *Divine Mystery*: these are
> the *company of Preachers, or of she-
> Preachers*, as the Hebrew speaks, who not
> by word, but by power appearing in them,
> put *Kings of Armies to flight.*

> —William Erbery (from *The Testimony
> of William Erbery Left Upon Record for
> The Saints of Succeeding Ages*, 1658)

> *So to me by an immediate revelation.*

> —Anne Hutchinson (attributed to her in
> *The Examination of Mrs. Anne Hutchinson
> at the Court at Newton*)

I wish to speak of "The Nonconformist's Memorial" as
a radical reading of the Gospels, or as a reading inspired by
the Gospel radicalism of Mary's usurpation of the apostolic
role—the root of churchdom. What we cannot help but call
the *actual* love of Mary for her saviour also makes her a
usurper; an unprecedented love upset foundations of the
nascent Church, displaced as the apostles were by an un-
canny diversion, her however momentary "turning" of the
gaze of divine belovedness from among the Twelve onto her
downturned and tear-filled eyes. Need we know more than
that "She," "some love-impelled figure," "was coming to
anoint him"; need we be more than her fellow anointers, in
all that the Lover of Jesus arrives in the night for—at the
Tomb from which dialogue and not nothingness ensues?

In looking closely at the Greek phrase from which *noli me tangere* ("do not touch me") is translated: *mē mou aptou*—we are able to see that the present-imperative case of the verb requires, literally, the translation "stop touching me." In his edition of the Gospel of John Raymond E. Brown translates the phrase as "Don't cling to me," a translation with which Susan Howe is familiar, as indicated on page 11 of *The Nonconformist's Memorial*. Insofar as Mary doesn't just reach for Jesus when he says her name, but *clings* to him until he speaks again: with his explicit qualification, then, of Mary's encounter with the risen Jesus as encompassing and indiscreet, as an encounter with the body neither dead in nor ascended from the flesh, but somehow free of death while yet in full abasement of the fatal wounds, does not John mean to say that it is Mary who is most intimate with the incarnation, if not penultimate to the resurrection— standing as she does in an unparalleled equilibrium with the miraculous? In contrast to the later, merely apostolic appearances—in that the appearance to Mary took place after the resurrection, but before the ascension—perhaps there is a type of ecstasy in the exchange between savior and self that is dependent on *Mary's* intent at the tomb, on *her* mantle of tearfulness rather than *their* complete surprise, on her differentiating of the fact of seeing the gardener from the act of being with Jesus at the sound, not of the *word* he gave, but of her given *name*.

Mary, unlike Thomas, fails to recognize Jesus not because she needs a sign, but because at first he doesn't call her by her name. In the *voicing* of her name, rather than in the speaking of a word or in the seeing of a sign, the lover of abasement is brought near. Whereas the apostles speak with caution, unassuredly, to a purified, hallucinatory Jesus given to walking through walls and to offering witness to symbolic wounds—wounds which, in Mary's arms, caused him pain enough, before he rose from the abasement that sustained them, to shrink from her reach and embrace—Mary, on the other hand, speaks assuredly to, and stands alone upon the still *ungodly* edge of resurrection, awaiting word of the eternal day of their impurity in being servants of mere love. The poet too is indeed this impure, this assured by the mysteries of love. In speaking in this interval between resurrection of the word and mere ascension from the flesh, the poet upholds no defense against the possibilities of beloving and being loved when it comes to words, ravishment of and by the other being focused momentarily in the search of both the poet for words of address, and of words for a form amidst chaos perhaps on her lips. "Not finding names there // Immanence is white with this":

> She saw herself bereft
>
> of body
>
> would only seem to sleep
>
> If I could go back
>
> Recollectedly into biblical
>
> fierce grace
>
> already fatherless
>
> Isled on all removes
>
> When night came on[2]

For Howe in this new night, the name is made of flesh, in that the flesh is what is scarred; it is the created word—and thus "bereft"—but what is searched-for is the creative word. Walter Benjamin says that "The deepest images of this divine word and the point where human language participates most intimately in the divine infinity of pure word, the point at which it cannot become finite word and knowledge, are the human name. The theory of proper names is the theory of the

---

[2] Susan Howe, *The Nonconformist's Memorial* (New Directions: New York, 1993), p. 32. [hereafter cited in text as N]

frontier between finite and infinite language."[3] Needless to say, Howe perhaps more than any other poet mines the mystical, transmigratory overlay of proper names. The appellative sedimentation from the depths of which those who populate her work—all perhaps Lazaruses—are resurrected, is in the first instance informed by, and therefore confirmation of a sometimes fierce, and sometimes pure experiment in the communicative and the absurd. But we experience such tenderness in being opened to the way in which this poet brings her foundlings in—brought closer to the meaning, then, or closer, even, to the pulse of naming than to that through which the search for truth can bring us. That it is actually not to our senses, but to our knees that we are brought by being witness to a name: this is the achievement, then, the actual urgency in a word by which we live.

Just as it at times explicitly rejects mediation, exceeding "the letter" as so many God-intoxicated writers since St. Paul have done, Susan Howe's "enthusiasm" tending toward silence, after Mary Shelley's dictum, often has recourse to an art supposing language capable of keeping one out of the reach of mediators, and thus of being miraculous in kind and not subordinate to immediacy as the only resistance to history. In this regard Howe is an avant-garde poet. She manages, however, to balance her art on a line adducible enough to produce true iconoclasm from violence, and still viable enough to divide materiality from mere critique. While she may be understood to celebrate language, insofar as—in echoing Mary's relations with Jesus at the Tomb—"It is the Word to whom she turns // True submission and subjection," Howe outdistances the avant-garde understanding of this celebration as an end-in-itself by exposing herself not just to language, but to the namer and the being-named to which, though free to speak, she still cannot but turn and cleave. The "Conversion" of the second half of *The*

[3] Walter Benjamin, "On Language as Such and on the Language of Man," *Reflections*, trans. Edmund Jephcott (Schocken Books: New York, 1978), p. 323-324. [hereafter cited in text as R]

Nonconformist's Memorial is truly a conversion (of) narrative, compelling what, like ecstasy, can only be called a counter to mediacy and text-centricity—the immortal and the materiality of language being those not quite mirroring termini from the dialectic of which, in nevertheless equal proportion, an abyss has been spun, but as if irrespective of all points of access still dissimilar from sources of heat. Within this dialectic between the infinite and finitude, between divinity and immanence, it is indeed specifically to the core of it—to the reconciliation in a Word made flesh—that poetry adds the necessary heat. In Howe's poems, but especially in "The Nonconformist's Memorial," God the Father and the Son of God—in a dialectic of the shepherding Word—at times become an unnamed figure for, or the source of a post-Holocaust theodicy of, the sourcelessness of pure hierarchy or immediacy of encounter in a fallen world, a world the virtuality of which is now compulsory: Howe challenges not just conservativism but even radical politics—and the very principle of politics—in relaying, while enunciating, news of a power beyond the reach of mediators, and, unlike politics, unmanipulatable at the level of language, like dictation in the Prophets is. Howe's courageous "complicity" in the radical tradition of prophetic divinity—and divine vicinity—manifests itself in the struggle for language, or the struggle against silencers, in the same way that, according to Walter Benjamin, Divine (non-lawmaking) Violence differentiates itself from Mythical (law-making) Violence in the process of history:

> Far from inaugurating a purer sphere, the mythical manifestation of immediate violence [as opposed to the violence of immediacy] shows itself fundamentally identical with all legal violence, and turns suspicion concerning the latter into certainty of the perniciousness of its historical function, the destruction of which thus becomes obligatory. This very task of destruction poses again, in the last resort,

the question of a pure immediate violence [immediate violence purified to a violence of immediacy] that might be able to call a halt to mythical violence. Just as in all spheres God opposes myth, mythical violence is confronted by the divine . . . If mythical violence is lawmaking, divine violence is law-destroying; if the former sets boundaries, the latter boundlessly destroys them; if mythical violence brings at once guilt and retribution, divine power only expiates; if the former threatens, the latter strikes; if the former is bloody, the latter is lethal without spilling blood.

Mythical violence is bloody power over mere life for its own sake, divine violence pure power over all life for the sake of the living. The first demands sacrifice, the second accepts it. (R 296-97 [my insertion])

Like Walter Benjamin, Howe identifies divinity with justice rather than worship or immortality, in accord with her vision of history as having been forced to profane its own sources in language and speech by an expropriating concept of knowledge, the essence of man. The poet struggles in an abyss between her thirst for a necessarily loveless, but unequivocally redeeming end of history, and aquiescence to the violence of history that love, while being pure, transcends only in passing or as a fugitive ultimately damned. Howe gestures toward pure hierarchy—or the suprahierarchical, above both legal violence, as Weber defined it, *and* essential love as mystics have experienced it. But in the same motion by which she nevertheless escapes subordination to the status quo of silencers in the throes of a violent love for ghosts who broke the law, the poet resurrects a love of God. In this especially physical acknowledgement of, or vigilance in anticipation of, not the autonomy of language as the end of closure, but heteronomy itself—the horizon of sound and demand—as godliness further from closure than any process, Howe more than any other poet takes the step that Emily Dickinson requires of those who seek where she alone once went, though it was not yet there: the theodicy, they say, is in the power and the fear; it is laid out—like Jesus in the Easter Tomb—by lineation in an ambit that, irreconcilable with all horizons, is endemic to a quest for God: the parousia enters now.

Prominent, then, in this dispensation of, not with, immediacy, is the emergence of, or else the circumstantiation of a non-intentional desire, "perfect primeval Consent," the foundling *volo* of a plunging heart. Language in the hands of mediators represses immediacy and chaos, and consigns us to utilization. Against this the poet of love establishes herself as a subject in relation to whom the fathering Word, as opposed to the premise of Fatherhood, speaks through the very fact that there is language to allot and through the fact that, though nothing, then, is any less unknown, our responsibility for language must, through the sincerity and inspiration of our use of it, nevertheless transcend the limits of it intrinsic to its having been posited and not received. Taggart too divulges in this process of exposing himself to language and the unknown the troubling role of a paternal force in relation to the act of composition. Both Howe and Taggart, like Abraham who answers "here I am," come to the act of composition already predisposed to being abolishers of immanence. Taggart's regard for the encounter with spiritual force is, in effect, the poetic counterpart to Simone Weil's existentialist faith as represented in "The Love of God and Affliction." But insofar as "enthusiasm" in Howe's poems remains true to its basis in the greek *entheos*: suffused with God—language in her use and sense of it is suffused with religious meaning, religious meaning being as ideologically distinct from the meaning of religion as the Johannine meaning of Word as the incarnation of God in the flesh, and of language as the flesh of Spirit presupposing resurrection of the Word but not the erection of a church, is lexically distinct from the propaganda of Acts and the Synoptic

Gospels. Because it contributed to Gnosticism the Gospel of John was among the last of the apostolic writings to be accepted into the canon of the Church Fathers. John, as legend has it, went on to design the Apocalypse, died a madman on Patmos and was taken up, like Elijah and Enoch before him, into heaven independently of the dialectic of life and immortality—a dialectic in which martyrdom was the particularly Christian stage of reconciliation at the time. Far from the crowds in Rome that, as legend has it, filled the first Catholic church at Peter's urging and convenient martyrdom, and under the lurid influence of an idea of the end of time as John the Baptist had announced it, and as John the Divine had then imagined it, a dream of wrath began to seethe counterhistorically to the Babylon that later radicals, the Puritans, would in fact identify with what became of Peter's churches under Constantine.

Howe and Taggart share with the martyrs and prophets this temptation to make an example of oneself and face the end. Influx in all manner of messages between devil and deity descends on a page. For in our heeding such a call as this the spirit decimates the means and ways, yet leaves a trace of the embrace upon our lips, as of a love supreme that somehow speaks. But if, in heeding, then, this spirit's spree of pain and bliss, we cannot find a way to live as we once did, then we may find ourselves confronted with what seems to be a fateful impatience with liberalism, and we might also see in ecstasy, as it upsets and speaks, and springs a sacred main, no more than a failure to deny authority, divine or not, its ties to a material life. Though the influx must come from outside, so too the sky in which the Father is thought to reside crosses the line between above and outside in a history of blood. Dominant among avant-garde poets, then, is a concern to deny the outside in order to avoid all accent of an orthodox sky. But more importantly: that which is otherwise than Being, or beyond essence, does not exist apart from self-destruction; only in this less limited—because less Eurocentric—sense of transformation can the Good beyond being be said to portend any pause, and to eventuate in a rectitude of which we cannot dream. While others may find it impossible to reconcile themselves as liberals to the fact that both Taggart and Howe are revising the Bible, I myself have been astounded in trying to measure the weight under which they must move in doing so as radically as they do. Immense and as intractable as the contradiction between prophetic historiography and encounter with war, and the idea of God that mystics have, as objectless desire, may be, we cannot but be profoundly moved in being witness to the processes by which both poets, but especially Howe as both a feminist and supplicant, must struggle toward resolution enough to allow for a willingness—not necessarily her own—to actually speak at all, or to be brought, therefore, to reckoning through the very voice of God to which—or to the power of which—the avant-gardists of our day attribute what is in fact their own control and tyranny over love.

Sounds pronounce a decree of concretion and vision sculpts fountains of sound on many pages of *The Nonconformist's Memorial*, especially in "A Bibliography of the King's Book, or Eikon Basilike," but to some degree in the title poem as well. In terms of the title poem, one might say that, typologically, as well as typographically speaking, an impulse often completes a kind of cycle from liquidity of thought to concretion of epic proportions. On what other scale than that of the path from the Easter Tomb in Palestine to the poet's desk past two millenia of silencing by the apostles; on what other scale than that of the path from Passion to the poet's tomb before which history rolled its wheelstones of both church and state, forcing night onto the page on which she "weeps to wake," as Percy Shelley said, the light and writes *I am;* on what other scale than that of the Prophets and Gospels reconceptualized in this way are we to witness this—one of the first truly radical returns of the spirit of prophecy in American poetry, if not since the 19th century, then since the final poems of Wallace Stevens—as it can only be witnessed: as spirit contradictorily embraced, reduced to nothing through millenia of avarice at the hands of its suppliers and benefactors right up through the

New Critics, and yet, through poetry itself, surmounting nothingness as such, to seize the day, the page, again and make that vantage sing.

The *Gnostic Gospel of Mary* further details the dialogue at the Tomb, and then depicts a confrontation between Peter and Mary Magdalene over the revelatory priority Mary claims to have been given over all men by Jesus the Son of Man. John Winthrop plays the role of Peter during the antinomian controversy in the New Canaan fifteen centuries later: "And that is the means by which she hath very much abused the country that they shall look for revelations and are not bound to the ministry of the word, but God will teach them by immediate revelations and this hath been the ground of all these tumults and troubles."[4] Anne Hutchinson, Eleanor Davies, Anne Lee, Joanna Southcott, Rebecca Jackson, and Emily Dickinson took a Magdalenian initiative against—a priorty over—Protestant orthodoxy, itself of course claiming spiritual priority over orthodox Catholicism *and* antinomian prophecy. I have spoken of the possibility of epic scale, but leave it off at this explicitly in regard to the legend of the New Testament Marys as a figure for the history of love that Susan Howe now speaks and resurrects. Howe and Mary speak across the gaping of a banishment completed over time, and yet without a change of scene: the empty tomb remains. The anointment, then, might otherwise depend on us, in following Howe across this last divide, in being touched by those lost souls for whom no seat outside the tomb is found, in being spoken to outside the tomb by those, within it there, who bear the burden of our being mute— who, unlike Jesus, still are born, give birth, and die inside a tomb.

Serpentine and self-begotten as the temptation of structure may be in an age enamored more with the absence of

---

[4] "The Examination of Mrs. Anne Hutchinson at the Court at Newton," *The Puritans in America* (Harvard Univ. Press: Cambridge, Mass. and London, England, 1985), p. 161.

God than with the victims of paradise, Howe in the first instance—by only paradoxically abjuring structure—succeeds in loosing a syllabic, yet conceptually tractable spell of re-allocation, urging through narrative not the fulfillment of proprietary impulse, but appropriation for the repulsed and dispossessed, and inviting scripture to put to the state-sponsored confines of the sacred the threat of a rent beyond compare and therefore irreparable. A rent effectively become the brink of allegory in a consciousness of loss is brought into relief against a backdrop of the miraculous, forming a pattern of awakening. A Hebraically prefigured advent of pneumatic collectivity is bestirred, that is, to no more cede itself to law by an at once both immanent and heteronomous speech-act: the spirited word polarized from empire by absurdity, by Tertullian's *credo quia absurdum* as heard through the speaking of Jesus from beyond the grave, in pentecosts, and from within the flesh as resurrection prompts the apostolic age at Mary's urging.

Expanding on Duncan's "line is in itself metaphor," each *page* is aligned as but a pentecost of itself, renouncing parity between the lines. Each page being like a site-specific but self-disengraving graph of articulations hitherto merely consubstantial with, and therefore, ultimately, indivisible from, inscrutability—that archimedean point to all prophetic cataloging and litany: each page as such affords us a view of, approach to, or consequence of, the Magdalenian gospel from behind eyes of prophets from Deborah to Dickinson, in light hiding the poet from our own eyes but shining on God.

> Resurrection and life are one
>
> it is I
>
> without any real subject
>
> all that I say is I
>
> A predicate nominative

> not subject the I is
>
> the bread the light the door
>
> the way the shepherd the vine
>
> (N 10)

Each page being encroached upon by silence is given lineaments enough to hold it up, as prophecy's archimedean point, to the fount of counterhistory's spelling out of justice at the omega now confined. One is faced with a kind of editorial decision in being confronted with the more concrete of these poem-pages: choosing either to merely look at the poem, foregrounding its graphology, or to reorient reading itself so as to keep up with the, at one level, irreducible vision, without losing ground to it in an elision of alternative, that is, ecstatic instrumentalities and meaning—"action," that is, not at the level of unity in the Aristotelian sense, but at a level perhaps including and yet always in some way other than, or more perilously possible than, the intentional and semantic. While it is important to perceive the vast proportions of materiality upon the page, if we are seeing what is literally there rather than following the lead of what reading affords us, then to whatever degree to which translation—as Benjamin understood it—takes its toll on sensory overload, the "face value" of these poem-pages does not by any means remain unrelativised: much more by way of a tendency toward meaning than by way of the inevitability of it, even in syllable-counts an impulse to narrative and argument is often set-loose through, rather than precluded by, the processes of elision and repetition, mirroring and concretion, rhythm and litany. Often when we say a word many words are said; words contain other words, not just many meanings. In the Jewish mystical tradition "notarikon" is a science of language-revelation based on this phenomenon of "words within words." Where Howe crosses words, sometimes doubling the availability of meaning, and at other times creating new levels of meaning or even gesturing paradoxically toward the meaning of meaning, wires cross at her feet where she reaps what the syllables sow and thus leaves an abyss. Leaving scars on, then unrolling scrolls, unfurling words and leaving none unturned, and none exempt from use, if not from love of words, Howe intends to say that there is meant to be a kind of expiation for our sins of meaning, which are based on what we expect from it, but at the same time a forsakenness not merely of the desire for meaning but of the freedom from chaos is legitimized, allowing for the possibility of tragedy. The emphasis of the elision and repetition, the mirroring and angularity of con-cretion here, falls not merely, and perhaps not at all, on a (conventional) critique of conventional instrumentality and meaning, but the burden of form—its being called upon by God—falls upon a mobilization of the possibility of meaning itself, both against its functions under patriarchy and capi-talism, but also in conjunction with the very meaning of its functioning at all. Howe laboriously reclaims the mecha-nism of meaning in its primacy as a metaphysics to which language extends the possibility of bodily contact, a meta-physics giving-way to rather than weighing-in against affec-tion and ecstasy in language.

The "Noli me tangere . . . "—"Touch me not; for I am not yet ascended to my Father: but go to my brethren . . . "—accentuates in this most breathtaking figure of desire in the West more of a tour-de-force, be it both feminist *and* pentecostal, through the outbreak of poetry taking its cue from a miracle, than it does by being miraculous itself and only figured as such in the service of dogma, the original metaphysical form of churchdom, churchdom being the handiwork that could only be of the denier of Jesus and Mary among the apostles. Certainly the 20th chapter of the Gospel of John means a great deal more to most of us as the source of the prologue to a poem by Susan Howe than it does as the centerpiece of the Christian resurrection myth. I find it hard to describe my reaction to the renewal that this poetic context—and Howe's poetic output in general—grants to scripture without ladening it, as poetry, with the requisite theoretical gaming of a neo-*via negativa*. Writing is religious, a re-*ligio* that, for those not yet by natural rights redeemed, thus circumstantiates an act of grace, maintaining peace but not at the expense of the war for equality. While some of us, like Susan Howe, may certainly harbor in our work an implicit, and even an ongoing, consideration of the Bible, the Bible itself, though highly unfashionable on the left, may in fact harbor a hermeneutic key to our search for the thus far elusive synchrony of history and ethics. The task of reinventing a theological idea of language, or, more simply, the orientation, now, of a prophetic turn in language must not, however, take hold of us under the influence or imminence of anything other than the possibility of a historical—as opposed to a discursive—dismantling of the New World Order.

Insight into the feminist political quest that Howe's work explores and in some way refounds, while legitimate and inspiring in its own right, should not leave one blind to Howe's commitment to scripture just because scripture is and has, since its inception, been used as a weapon by the very oppressors against which she is striving as a woman. Just as the papists and fundamentalists are blind to the provisional nature of biblical language, and deaf to the prophetic message defying them to deny their own power as mediators, radical critics and poets are prone to reductive presumptions as well, often finding themselves confused or thrown off course by what might best be described as Howe's insubordinating rematerialization of the lore and metaphor of prophetic monotheism. We have a great deal to learn from Howe's hermeneutic access to the Prophets and the Gospels—as much about the repressed messages of the Bible as we do of our own presumptions about prophecy and gospel in precluding them from the very same political quest that Howe, in willing tandem with scripture, more courageously—because paradoxically—undertakes for us at this most dangerous time. I have said, and without undue qualification, that Howe is a religious poet, and that her religion of poetry is "prophetic" in the most relevant sense of the word—relevant, that is, insofar as a vision of history is uttered in verse, which *re*-verses the history of scripture in seeking the Tomb, to commune with the Word. Only Mary weeps at the Tomb, and Renan says that only this weeping—what all appearances of the Holy Spirit presuppose—lives on in the scripture that stills it beginning with Acts.

Howe's work sustains a complex, almost formidable "return of the repressed" in terms of the 19th century as well. But in her eyes Melville and Dickinson come forward as the sources for our reconsideration of prophecy and of the role of poetry, Whitman and Emerson finally being left behind by a major American poet.[5] This is a crucial step that Howe has taken for us as far as poetics goes—leading us out from under the burden with which organicism and ego-worship have saddled our assessment of Democracy and our perception of progress. The wanton rejection of alterity and sacrifice in American ideology most certainly presupposes such a profitable—and marginalizing—burden of assent. As inspiring and significantly erudite as Robert Duncan was—and not withstanding Howe's acknowledged indebtedness to him—even in sublimating psyche, he still presumes himself to be expanding on a subjectivity, an ego-construct of the view that his voice affords us of history and cosmos. Toward an aftermath of Romantic desire as Duncan so generously understood it, on the other hand, we, being the young, have been forced at this time to mislead ourselves even further—brought as never before to the point of being led headlong, and in hordes, into a divide on every side of which a silence has begun to reign. In this divide resides the ethical relation. Unearthed asymmetries shadowing immanence, and in fact

[5] Recently Howe gave a series of compelling lectures on Melville at SUNY Buffalo, and her work with and against Olson's patriarchal reading of Melville—who is not, claims Howe, a founder but a foundling—remains ongoing, most recently finding expression in the monumental, yet open-ended "Melville's Marginalia" in *The Nonconformist's Memorial*. In terms of Dickinson of course, her *My Emily Dickinson* remains exemplary of all that scholarship and poetry might have in common in the context of a distinctly American spiritual and linguistic consciousness.

capacitating the very disgrace that we must finally make of it, take shape in magnanimity and abasement at this time. We are forced to deduce, then, from the very specter of the violence to which Duncan was so vastly a witness in his war poems, the possibility of the fact that a primary source of such violence may lie in the very instance of having a view in the first place, of widening an "I" the centrism of which might paradoxically serve as a macrocosmic paradigm for indifference and marginalization in history and the ecosphere. Insofar, that is, as Duncan, and so many of the other New American Poets of whom Howe and Taggart are the most important heirs, remain, to a certain extent, resolutely psychical in their conceptions of intersubjectivity in history and the ecosphere, perhaps they simply overcome, or remain unaccountable to, the demands that in Howe's writing are made on, and by, the material of a language that is experienced as a redistributive tribunal, rather than as a shifting "code" in an analogy with dream material or in a *mūthos* of collective drift.[6] Again the movement from the life of the psyche to the promise of life must be effected in the decision of prophecy. Howe has made this decision: afflicted by mystery rather than transported by it; silenced by the music of the spheres rather than composing in accordance with it;

[6] The works of Duncan, Olson, Spicer, Dorn, and Robin Blaser remain central to most poetic discourses and practices of the sacred and of history that exist today. If not in the historical sense in which the works of the Modernists are such milestones, I am still tempted to accord to the work of these later poets a significance equal to, or even greater than that of the Modernists. The movement in our culture toward a neo-centralized, illiterate technocracy, however, permits of no refusal, on the part of the young, to go to different extremes of the sacred and the historical than those toward which the cold-war visionaries went: furtherance in this regard entails a linking of heteronomy, language, and receptivity in such a way as we have only hinted at in theory, but have in some instances even tended toward in practice, under the influence of the New American Poetry. Indeed Howe and Taggart remain part of a tradition in which they are nevertheless opening new dimensions of theory and practice, in accord with the changing nature of the socio-political imperatives of our time.

holding-forth hopelessly against (the myth of) progress yet diminishing its stature even as she is overcome by it; seeking not to understand the nature of Being but to be worthy of it; finding not cyclical conciliation, but rejection and excess, in the specter and the messages of "process"—Howe, like Melville and Dickinson before her, and like the English and New England antinomians before them, begins again to reshape the horizon of verse into a prospect of conversion, breaking the limits of language into kindling for fires of a love victorious over foes of nomadism.

Melville tells us that there will be a conflict between consciousness, the availability of self, and conscience, the overcoming of our self-sufficiency, forever registering its pendulum swings like battle-cries in the deepest recesses of our mortality. If consciousness founds the monological order with which only the conscience it explicity represses is still irreconcilable, then conscience reconciles shared endeavor with desire by inspiring anarchy, pure hierarchy, objectless desire. In *The Blue Book* Wittengstein asks, "but do we interpret the words before we obey the order," rhetorically implying that language is perhaps constitutive not just of consciousness but of the will as well; language insofar as it is systematic not only "contains" the thought process, but circumstantiates and therefore to no uncertain degree determines our decisions as well. But Moses in the wilderness of Exodus guides his kin, when faced with the fiery propsect of heteronomous responsibility for the promise of life, toward a refrain approximated in the words "we will do and we will hear"—the Hebrew conjunction in this case implying a linearly temporal as well as formally differentiating relationship between "doing" and "hearing." Profoundly and paradoxcially in terms of the very structure of biblical language, then, the burden of what later constitutes the way of "faith,"—Luther's *sola fides*—comes to life if we are wont, or simply able, to do God's will *before* it becomes "known" to who does so, to obey the call before the words that constitute it are heard, to respond to what calls only in precedence to the very principle of mediation underlying language and knowledge—in precedence, that is, to that which makes of all dialogue, and for that matter all response, an agent of identity rather than sacrifice, dialectic rather than collectivity.[7]

Finally taking for granted the proximity of Patmos to Shiloh and Moscow, but without relying on the coincidence of the year of the Bolshevik uprising with the 19:17 of Revelation which Howe quotes as the epigraph to the second part of "The Nonconformist's Memorial," we can begin to take measure of the furious historicity of Howe's engagement with the biblical, specifically in terms of the political and counterhistorical implications of apocalyptic religion. That is, in terms of the formal and thematic violence at times either wandering in her work, as fabled masterlessness, or else reflected in the writing process historiographically, it is perhaps impossible not to recognize the provocation that, in "grounding" the excess, in sovereignly sending us back, she sets before us at the urging of this book—Revelation being, with Daniel, among the most important texts upon which the Radical Reformation, fueled by the idea of law-destroying, sovereign violence, was founded in the princedoms of

[7] In one of his *Nine Talmudic Readings* Levinas describes the temporal paradox of the "and" in "we will do and we will hear" as the "temptation of temptation": faith is the tempting of knowledge to deny its own temptation of the heart. Levinas in a later work, *Otherwise than Being or Beyond Essence*, explains that "this inwardness without secrets is a pure witness to the inordinateness which already commands me, to give to the other taking the bread out of my own mouth, and making a gift of my own skin." He comes to base, by implication, his phenomenology of a reversed asymmetry of the relation between self and other on the paradox of faith, given the supreme example of it as depicted in Exodus. Standing in oblique relation to Hebraic revelation as it is understood by Levinas, Benjamin's radically German Romantic theory of language in "On Language as Such and on the Language of Man," a brilliant reading of Genesis and the creation of language, depends on a complex distinction between word and name, having to do with the fact that God gave *word* of Man but made him *name* the world.

Bohemia and Saxony, and consummated, within an Anglo-American tradition, in the departure of the Mayflower and the beheading of King Charles I. Though much has been said about Marx's critique of religion, a critique that is only slightly less reductive than Freud's, what little has been said about the socio-religious historical context (millenarian/millenialist Britain, 1848) in which, though perhaps more under Engel's influence, the *Communist Manifesto* appeared, does not fully account for the contradiction of a Communist apocalypticism—its deviance in light of Marx's own supposedly secular terms of socio-economic, rather than Providential determination in history, as expounded in *Das Kapital.* Others like Ernst Bloch later seized on the very terms of consummation by which we cannot fail to, in part, identify the *Manifesto*—which was written at the height of, and in day to day contact with both post-Cromwellian millenarianism and Utopian/ Enlightenment millenialism—as a messianic document: not only, that is, as a scientistic inroad of the bridge to the classless supremacy that historical materialism placed between the proletariat and his feats, but also as a product of religious consciousness politicized to the degree to which its eschatological historical vision was internalized to make it work in every "working man," to rematerialize the workers' rights in every sphere of life not yet destroyed by immortality or the right to own. As usual more than a century ahead of his time, Kierkegaard, unlike Marx, is already prepared to confront and necessarily redirect the paradox of a secular millenium. At the moment of the *Manifesto* in Britain, of the failed European revolutions, and of the revolutionary way in which Melville begins—in the Man-of-War World of *White Jacket* that gives rise to the Leviathan at war with Man in *Moby-Dick*—to be rent asunder in finding, finally, the knife-edge of history in the distinction between failed revolutions (in Europe), and the failure of a revolution won (America's): in heeding the moment, that is, of what for many historians has become a final piece in the puzzle of Western decline, on what was supposed to be the hither side of history Kierkegaard utters the curse that Anglo-American sectarianism had long since come to fulfill. In terms of radical religion on the right and left, of course, this may be the curse that liberalism cannot survive:

> What lay at the root of the catastrophe [the European Revolutions] will then become apparent, that it is the opposite of the Reformation, which appeared to be a religious movement and proved to be political; now everything appears to be politics but will turn out to be a religious movement.[8]

Sussurium Cum Deo

No one seems to be willing to concede even the slightest bit of legitimated critical space to the possibility of a prophetic rather than a neo-pragmatist or deconstructive transformation registered in the writing process of poetry. Perhaps the distinction of which I am speaking—left unattended for now—is one between a counterhistory and a non-

---

[8] Soren Kierkegaard, *Journals and Papers*, ed. and trans. Edward V. Hong and Edna H. Hong (Indiana Univ. Press: Bloomington, 1978), p. 60. [my insertion]) Kierkegaard later incoporates this idea/prophecy into the third preface (written in the aftermath of the failed revolutions of 1848) of his *On Authority and Revelation: the Book on Adler, or a Cycle of Ethico-Religious Essays*: "And then when this provisional convulsive phase has been passed through and the *political* ministers are gone, the race will be so tired out with sufferings and loss of blood that this thing of eternity might get permission at least to be taken into consideration, as to whether it might not, from the very first, heat passion anew and give it new powers. The reaction (conversely to that of the Reformation) will transfigure what seemed to be, and imagined itself to be, politics into a religious movement. To get eternity again requires blood, but blood of a different sort, not the blood of thousands of warriors, no, the precious blood of martyrs, of the individuals—the blood of martyrs, those mighty dead who are able to do what no living man can do who lets men be cut down by the thousands."

absorption. It is indeed the very possibility of counterhistory that I sense most clearly, and with great incentive, in reading poems by Susan Howe. Her work with the fascicles of Dickinson seems to have prepared her to confront her masters, History and Deity, in the very struggle with which the Romantics and the Modernists had left her until *Articulation of Sound Forms in Time*. In the later work a distinct, if irrecoverable type of momentum, or a momentum of typology in this struggle has made itself known to us as a quest for God.

In directly repressing the possibility of spirit that her work commands and answers-to, much of the critical response to this work has been, in turn, as forcefully evasive of the tenor of her prophetic "voice" as it has been careless in its reinscription of her textual methods into a limited avant-garde poetics. The fragment in Howe's work is not by any means merely a marker of non-teleology, or a banner of exile, but rather it is a consequence of non-linguistic power over form. That which has shorn the fragment is unmanifest, but still in contrast to the face of God. The fragment is sacred; it is the consequence not of a radical dismantling of content, but of a decimation of language by absolute content. Just as the historical repressions under logocentrism in the West—the repressions with which the most interesting critics and poets are so eminently concerned—are violent in their attempt to sustain normative hierarchy and value-systems in our society, the "acceptance" of Howe's work by the literary avant-garde is, in effect, a nearly Hegelian ploy of avant-garde identity, a containment, at the level of form, of what is threatening to the avant-garde at other levels of this radically inspired and uncompromising work. The limited avant-garde identity into which Howe's work fits only in terms of the *appearance* of its concretizations at the level of the page represses, as all identity must, the quest for God in which her language implicates itself, iconoclastically, by disavowing form. There is strong irony in the fact that critics and poets have been quick to rally around Howe's critique of knowledge without facing the demands of the possessing spirit for which those victims that she has "lifted tenderly" from history were themselves condemned in the name of reason. Even in seeming to concur and elaborate upon her rage against the atrocities of hierarchy and knowledge, the rationalist condemnation of the threat to hierarchy that inspiration poses continues to live-on even in the most supposedly anti-Enlightenment tenets of these responses— not in the outright sense of a John Winthrop banishing the prophetic feminine from New England, but more subtly in acts of evasion and elision of charisma and the possibility of revelation.

Why shouldn't we speak of the possibility of prophecy in terms of Howe's work, and thus admit that her vision of history owes more to the ideas of God which fueled revolts from history than it owes to the tradition of "historicism" that presupposes atheism and the supremacy of reason. Certainly she shares with Taggart an intensity of purpose, a prospectus for the speech-act presupposing encounter with, or else defiance in alliance with, the Holy Spirit as depicted, in descending, in the Book of Acts. As poet-pentecostals they in fact refuse to surrender the possibility of spirit, of heteronomous influx, Benjamin's Divine Violence, to those in the employ of whom, through myth and law, it comes to sponsor only avarice even *after* the shedding of blood. But neither do they concede, to those who merely resist it, any letting-up in the spiritual encounter itself. As repulsed parishioner in the church of Jazz, as listener disinterred into the grip of Soul, Taggart casts all our denial and belatedness aside as so much programmatic chaff at harvest-time, composing Kierkegaardian solos for our own and his accompaniment in the searchings of Coltrane and Ayler, of Marvin Gaye in *What's Goin On*—all insurgent heirs to the paradox-gospel, all as though sons of the blood-bodily love, of an "illegitimate Father."

By all appearances the poems in *Loop* and the poems in *The Nonconformist's Memorial* are not of a piece, or at least not of the same piece as that by which the Prophets and

Gospels bind these poets at a referential level. But while both poets, following Duncan and Olson at their most magisterial, reckon with the possibility of providing meta-prosodic structure, careful attention to minute progressions at a syllabic level is the constant of composition in both cases. Contrary to what is ostensibly so unique about the poems in *Loop*, to what may nevertheless remain Taggart's "signature" device, I am convinced that Taggart's lines tend less toward an assent to repetition than toward a condition of unrest that is nevertheless always in the process of, but never not in some way at the mercy of, resolution insofar as it is heteronomous. Just as restlessly, but perhaps *against* the possibility of there even being a "condition," Howe's lines, on the other hand, like new kindling under a hitherto only represented ire—an ire first felt in Constitutional America by Melville—"sire" a kind of fellowship between expletive and litany. In a pendulum swing of pure hierarchy between dirge-like prosodic grapplings and breakthroughs of inarticulable affection, Howe goes about the task of registering counterhistory in typeface and singing. However different hymnody and discant may be from litany, permutation from glossolalia, in light of any serious concern for the content of Howe's and Taggart's poems there can be no doubt that kinship in their plundering of the Prophets and Gospels is a reality beyond question, and especially beyond the question of form that looms perhaps divisively over any attempt at reading these ostensibly so different collections as though they were of a piece. Of course neither poet is in any sense conventional; both are in their own way operating on the margins of today's mainstream tradition, if one can call it that, while at the same time exposing themselves to the heterodox, largely Protestant religious tradition rejected by the dominant mainstream *and* oppositional poetry worlds alike. The relative lack of critical interest in Taggart's work, more than on anything else a comment on the trend-oriented failure of criticism per se—its blindness to achievements that cannot be accounted for wholly on its own methodological terms, with their requisite timeliness—may in turn be accounted for surely in terms of Taggart's explicitly permissive—in Duncan's sense of "permission"—if combative poetics of decision before the tribunal of spiritual force.[9] Taggart demands too much both of readers for whom spirit is not an issue and of readers for whom it is the only issue. But whereas these demands—involving complex musical and philosophical structure, zero-point syllabic tracery, and Ezekiel-like, more inviolable than violent, visions of influx— on readers for whom spirit is not an issue are themselves rejected, rather than accepted as legitimate but admittedly not lived-up to, it is only in meeting such extreme demands as these that readers for whom spirit is real are able to perceive at all. The certitude of those few who follow Taggart's doings borders on being a scourge to both deser- tion *and* massacre at the scene of writing. We need hardly be surprised by the fact that among the undeniably major poets of our time, Susan Howe is one of the few who are willing to meet these demands; in fact she does so overwhelmingly in her work, not in resisting the premises of Taggart's vision, which she in part shares with him, but in mirroring the consequences of its terrorism and its quite possibly methodi- cal compositional force with her own terror as a prophetess for whom language, though not methodically so, is, like Taggart's "voice that eats the face away," a descendent of "transfiguration beyond gender" and "perfect primeval Consent." Without explicitly reiterating the Romantic reconceptualization of prophecy as dictation, a reconcep- tualization that often posits a "muse" as the agent of influx rather than God as its origin, both Taggart and Howe do reiterate, but without simply returning to prophecy in the ancient sense either, the possibility of non-intentional desire

[9] In this regard see especially the poem "Not Quite Parallel Lines," and the poetics-pieces ("Were You" and "Lab Notes") in *Loop*. See also his statement on the relation of jazz to his work at the back of *Prompted* (Kent State University Libraries, 1991) for a further description of spiritual encounter during the writing pro- cess, as well as his new book, *Remaining in Light* (SUNY Press), for a revisionary reading of Edward Hopper as a painter of potentially revelatory encounter.

and encounter, often in the process of overcoming hierarchy with sound. As intention and perspective are subjected to repetition and chaos, the suprahierarchical—the objectlessness of a desire continuously unrestored to itself, or the self-replacing objectlessness of absolute desire—comes down as a content of sound.

Distinctions between the poetries of Howe and Taggart come most fruitfully to bear in our perception of the particular political and existential value of their different "methods" of non-conformism, such methods being relative, of course, to the nature of their sources and to the project of our resistance as poets in general. What are the ramifications of their language experiments in regard to the problematic ontological and epistemological structures from which they more or less intentionally differentiate the writing process and the role of language? Is this crucial attempt at differentiation from the logocentric itself the watershed for our evaluation of the political or ethical importance of these books? In a review of *Peace on Earth*,[10] one of Taggart's earlier and most extraordinary books, Howe herself found it difficult to relinquish the hold her pessimism had on her nevertheless attentive reading of the book so that she might follow suit in the exhortation to passional community that the title poem offers us. Howe implies that the hymn-like quality of the poems in *Peace on Earth* bestirs an optimism that might be irreconcilable with the quest for justice that, though in great sympathy at the level of content, the poems hold-forth formally in a cycle that renounces chaos. But Taggart believes that repetition is itself a kind of language, one that, unlike more transparent forms, atones for its own mediacy, foregrounding decision and carrying forward from form the much forbidden step of resignation: the onus of what, for the one without more, is in store at the heart of a word.

[10] "Light in Darkness: John Taggart's Poetry," *Hambone* 2 (Spring 1982), p. 135-138.

Divine Madness

The God of the prophets is invoked as a foe of the
annihilators of nomadism. The Stuart Translators of the
Gospel of Luke were of course already Christians, already
others in a long line of debauching interpolators beginning
with Paul, when, in rendering Luke's attribution of the
saying "the Kingdom of God is within you" to Jesus, they
chose the word "within" over the other form of the prepo-
sition in question, that being embodied in English by the
word "among"—the "you" in this case being a pronoun not
of interiority, in the singular as Paul would have it, but of a
polity quite literally at risk. Over the Authorized Version,
based in part on the Latinate Bishops' Bible, a lectern bible
if there ever was one, the Puritans preferred the Geneva Bible
translated by Marian Exiles under the influence of Calvin-
ism, with its decisively demotic apparatus and its anti-papal
marginalia.[11] Conformed by way of the unorthodox, if not
Gnostic theology of the Johannine Redactor—a theology
following upon the ascension of Jesus to his *pre-existent*
rather than his now attained-to and salvific seat beside the
Throne—the apostle John, it seems, is represented as having
only *interpolated* into Jesus's confrontation with Pilate the
stoicism of "my kingdom is not of this world," not having
entered into the Judgment Hall himself on account of
Passover restrictions.[12] Not "my kingdom is not of this
world," but rather "your empire is destroying my world," is

[11] Though he made it possible, King James never "authorized"
the Bible named for him; its dependence on Tyndale's translations,
on which the Geneva Bible also depended, certainly must have
seemed amiss considering James's bleak antipathy for the Geneva
Bible.

[12] Ernst Bloch premises his essay "Christian Social Utopias," in
Man On His Own, on a catalogue of such contradictions as these.
He believes that Christianity is itself a development out of the
contradiction between a prophetic message and the message of
immortality, both of which Jesus brought to the Jews and Gentiles
of his time.

what, in keeping with the socio-economic underpinnings of even his most life-threatening flourishes—those of apocalypse, the saviour must at that deciding moment have said. In refusing to hierarchicalize immortality Jesus strove radically against the possibility of any stoic hermeneutic on the part of those devoted to him but destined, he knew, for things far less sacred than reform. From the cross in the gospels according to Matthew and Mark, Jesus reckons with his immortality in uttering a radical curse, a Copernican revolution, if you will, of the incarnation. Following Psalm 22, to which Jesus remains most fully connected in the icons and altarpieces of Northerners, both Catholic and Quietist, before the Enlightenment, the pose of mortal immortality hitherto limited to hope, patrilinearly pigeonholed, though now no longer populated by ministering and beatitude, but by a mystery of, and vengeance for the dying, and an answer for the long-since dead: *Eloi, Eloi, lama sabachthani (my God, my God, why hast thou forsaken me)*—is followed through the Passion, then, not heavenward as yet, but to the core of exposure itself as the only end. The word is a curse. The paradox of prophecy rests in part on the seeming contradiction in the fact that voices of the highest stature in the Bible return more often to the subject of our nothingness as a species than to any other theme, more often, even, than they mourn for what as a species we reduce to nothing; and yet, at the same time, and for the first time, they throw into profound relief, ecstatically against a backdrop of visions of both a paradise surpassed and future doom, the falsehoods upon the basis of which flowering anthropocentrism is in fact more misanthropic than prophecy.

Only in keeping with this most remote possibility of prophecy, remote, that is, in indirect proportion to the degree to which it has been posited and not received, is there to be a place accorded us—not beyond time, but by a promise led beyond us into life. Micah condemned those prophets who predicted good fortune for the more generous and misfortune for the more parsimonious of their employer kings. King Ahab called Elijah a mischief-maker and a destroyer of the very people whose doom the prophet predicted expressly for the purpose of saving them from Ahab. Though most passionately possessed by the jealousy of YHWH toward the kings, Elijah, like Abraham before him and Amos after, shows himself at other times to be a protector of the people from such jealousy when taken to lengths beyond what was necessary for reform. The prophet Samuel may be favored with the description of being the first of the Nebiim ecstatics—charismatic war-oracles to the desert confederacies—to in part break with the pattern of prophetic complicity in establishmentarian interests, as manifested in the demand for warrior-ecstasy and oracular policy-making, which, for the purposes of supporting a growing Israeli war-machine, became during the royalist period increasingly internalized against a native peasantry consigned to duty in the struggle of the kings for world power. Although the royalist tradition hallowed Samuel as a Nabi whose works and words belonged in the lineage of warrior-kingship prophecy beginning with the Nazarites, in the anti-royalist, confederate peasantry tradition, he is credited with having litanied, for the future of prophecy, a description of the kingship's turning back of the deliverance from slavery—turning away as kings do from the face of God to place in bondage both the peasantry within and the enemy outside their regimes: by the appointment of the sons of Israel, some as horsemen for his chariots, running before them as animals, others as weapon builders in times of war and reapers of his fields in times of peace; by the appointment of the daughters of Israel as his cooks and cake-makers; by the commandeering of the fields and vineyards of the children of Israel; by the creation of fiefdoms to support the expansion of his political apparatus and influence, etc… the King shall be proven a Pharaoh—"And ye shall cry out in that day because of your king which ye shall have chosen you, and the Lord will not hear you in that day." (1 Sam. 8:18.)

Internecion

With the incursion, in public, of a specifically auditory character of revelation and therefore of divinity, as manifested among the classical prophets of the Bible, coincided a kind of dehiscence in the meeting-point of history and the infinite, which is the point at which the very principle of public prophecy indeed re-covenanted, as historicity itself, the word of God in absolutizing ethics and the sacrifice of self. But by the phrase *dehiscence in the meeting point of history and the infinite*, I also mean to indicate the vision of Ezekiel. In the paranormality, if not the ecstasy, of the prophetic sojourn before the polity—an excursion in radical spokenness—we are confronted with a speech-act constructed at, yet conflating, the levels of origin, utterance, meaning, and reception in a way that is unique to the biblical tradition. For it is on the tongues of the prophets that a witnessing to history is pronounced, not in the name of God, but as a permutation of the God they name. We are witness to a breaking-forth of heteronomy from the chains of gestation and mediacy produced by the powers of representation—a breaking-forth suffusively that, though radical in its time, ultimately led to Paul's pneumatic reconceptualizaion of revelation as election, and of election as the very irreconcilability of faith and history, of God and language—this irreconcilability being the very premise of salvational orthodoxy in Catholicism, a premise that even Jesus, as socio-centric as his teachings were, could not recoil from according to the Gospel of John. Pauline Christianity between the Resurrection and the monk Joachim, in Augustine's authoritative version of it, rendered prophecy useless, trapping it between two ages in the process of disincarnating the millenium as Daniel and John the Divine had conceived it, and as Eusebius understood it: as an imminent presupposition of, rather than an ideal opposition to, the unfolding of history in the flesh.[13] Though repressed

---

[13] Joachim of Fiore, born in 1135 in Calabria, almost single-handedly reintroduced apocalyptic spirituality into the exegetical

during the time between the return from the Babylonian exile and the birth of John the Baptist—repressed, that is, by priestly reforms under Ezra to make way for the Canon and the Law of the Scribes—"Ruach," or "Spirit," first enters the lexicon of prophecy consistently in the words of Ezekiel and Second Isaiah; but only in the prophecy of Joel does it, in the apostles' eyes, become a "type," with Peter's recognition of the Lord's "pouring out of my spirit upon all flesh," in the second chapter of the Book of Joel, as the model for their pentecostalism. In all of the Old Testament only this passage could legitimize the tendency toward mass-ecstasy that, at the birth of Christianity—and then throughout the history of the millenarian, non-Augustinian reconceptualization of it at the urging of Joachim—served as the instrument of God in the public domain. Early Christian prophecy, that is, stood in contrast to the solitary forms that, in the pre-exilic sound and countenance of Hebrew prophecy, were given shape to as the voice of God by pariahs and not demagogues. During the time of canonization following the return from exile, the relegation of the prophetic impulse to the past, or rather the prohibition of the future for which prophecy calls, reaches its culmination in the self-repressing prophecy of Zechariah: "And it shall come to pass, that when any shall yet prophesy, then his father and his mother that begat him shall say unto him, Thou shalt not live; for thou speakest lies in the name of the Lord: and his father and his mother that begat him shall thrust him through when he prophesieth."(13:3). The pre-exilic scriptural prophets had avoided the term *ruach* in order to differentiate themselves from the Nabi (warrior-ecstasy) tradition, the complicity of

process, and, more importantly, into the language of the laity for whom Saint Francis became the second Christ. Though almost universally dominant in the Church since Augustine, the individualizing and moralizing interpretation of Revelation was nevertheless definitively, if only subculturally, challenged by popularizations of Joachim's eschatological rereading of temporal history into the script. Radical Protestantism in England, and the errand of the Puritans into the wilderness of New England were premised, of course, on such a standard of apocalyptic historiography as well.

which was overcome, beginning with Elijah, in a turn away from internecine dream-reading, magic, and deification, toward poetry and ethics on a universal scale. But with its return from exile and its integration into a Persian and then a Hellenic Empire, the Jewish *ruach*, and more precisely, Second Isaiah's *ruach ha kodesh*—holy spirit—again showed promissory signs in public ecstasy and in the reading of dreams as the career of Daniel would redefine it—in terms, that is, of an apocalyptical redefinition of what "reading" and "dreams" actually are.

The singularity of Biblical prophecy as an exemplar of a particular type of religion, that being monotheism, resides less in its outright rejection of Mediterannean nature religion than it resides in a prominence given to the auditory break-through found to be wanting in epiphanic and pantheistic ritualism. While the rejection of nature worship is to some extent implied by auditory breakthrough at the level of language, in Biblical prophecy the foregrounding of voice and language, the only means by which community becomes supplied, indicates not simply a new forum for authority over nature, but an acute historical consciousness of the compromise with which the sacredness of nature had been wracked by the decline of nomadism. Perhaps all paradox, even those paradoxes of which language is at certain times the symptom and at others the source, stems from this initial attempt to intervene—in establishing language itself as both the face and revelation of a God in history—in the supremacy of proprietary authority over nature and beings with supreme authority over proprietors as the meaning of history.

In the first instance prophecy effects a paradoxical locutionary reversal in which the issuing of an order is coincidental to and in fact uniquely inextricable from the signification of a reception of it by the one who obeys. The transcendence of what is obeyed by a prophet is erected on the basis of the way in which the epiphany arrives only in the saying of the one who receives it. Only prophecy allows for the arrival of an order to which I am subjected before hearing it, *or which I hear in my own saying*. The call first founds itself in Abraham, whose name is "here I am." The name of "here I am" in which, from the first, the one who is here exists only in the accusative, is not the answer to, but an exponent of, the call. Milton's sonnet on the massacre of the Waldenses at Piedmont is prophetic precisely for its locutionary method, not for its polemical status. Not as the response of a partisan, antiphonal to a martyrdom which is itself at stake, but as an exponent or redoubling of the prophetic call of, which is itself of sufferers to, a withdrawing God, does the suffering intrinsic to every call become the thing set-off and then fleshed-out in Milton's poem.[14] In near identification with a diachronic call, and in being an exponent of, and not antiphonal to, the word of God, the voice of prophecy is brought to bear at different levels, but in a single offering of signs, or in a sign of the offering of signs.

Abraham disrupts familiality in binding Isaac for a sacrifice of kind. The sacrifice of kind reconstitutes the heteronomy from which fecundity itself must spring. All remittance of the coming to life of his capacity as a progenitor to give a sign, identify, and thus originate the gift, lies dormant in the binding time until a knife is raised. *This allegiance before any oath, this responsibility prior to commitment, is precisely the other in the same, inspiration and prophecy, the passing itself of the Infinite.* The Infinite first passes itself, not from a position beyond which it no longer surrounds us, but, more starkly even than in our absence, by virtue of an imposition on (and not an opposition to) continuous identity. Beyond rather than between the poles of even the most momentary or monumental divide, the Infinite passes itself as it enters the space of a sacrifice during the time that it takes for a knife to descend. Only a tear in the eye of one who raises it can outshine the gleam on such a

---

[14] Nick Lawrence, in conversation, has emphasized the word "redoubling" in describing the locutionary method of this poem.

blade. In the promissory economy of the departure of faith, the son, as a sign not of God, but of woman and man, is an emphasis placed on the Fall. That the child must, both in theory and practice, improve upon the paternity of God—the principle of creation—to become a father, marks in the course of what is therefore only an appropriative repetition of that primal day, the pursuit of an insuperable homogeneity: the patriarchal line. Our resistance, since the beginning of recorded history, to the alienability of ownership is symptomatic of this insuperability of the link between homogeneous self-consciousness (the "unhappy," non-homogeneous version of which Hegel describes as the Jewish source of the Jews' own persecution within the more or less homogeneous ontologies of the Greeks, the Romans, and especially the Christians) and the total dominion of consciousness over that which does not presuppose it—over that which, were it not for rights of ownership, it would be completely without: in a state of non-identity, *in the trace of a wandering cause.*

The God of the prophets, whose name has been, as acronym, the act of binding all the signs, demands the sacrifice of all that mortals only *necessarily* signify. Beyond what is only necessarily signifiable, but in profound relation to this necessity—to the *conatus essendi* of all beings, of all that "is"—awaits a significance of what is not just unnecessary, but of what is impossible. Although invoked by the claim of a literal exteriority, and by the literal claim of the neighbor in need, the entry of the non-indifference of, on the hither side of immanence, the "here I am" into discourse is necessarily brought to an end in the utterance of "am." Outside of discourse, or rather, continuously caught in an offering no longer of signs, whatever "is," and is always the same, exists only for the debt of this "is," and is, because of this, predeterminately accused—in the accusative as in the Abrahamic "here I am"—and called-forth on a course of interminable solicitude. Solicitude may be called a coming-forth of one's difference from but non-indifference toward, or a consubstantial longing and responsibility for, what, as the other, is never the same, and not ever an "is." Returning only as a poetry in this pattern of both longing and solicitude, another origin begins to loom: if we are bold enough to call into question, rather than simply redistribute the category of the masculine, then a disruption at the divide of the feminine—the prophetic feminine from beyond and otherwise independent of any essence, further from closure than any process, more absent than nothingness, yet more irrepressibly constitutive than the materiality of nature—enters into all continuums as a scourge, and into discord as a salve. Counteracted are our returns on the investments of identity and dialectics, for these are the investments upon which Western civilization is based—investments within the continuity of which the other is always a provision for, and never a recipient of, the gift of life. In neither the trajectory nor the epiphany of a rage borne by the "here I am" toward all periplums, two witnesses to human maternity and parricide coincide to be the eyes of a prophetess offering signs. Upon the ethical is necessarily based this leap into a distinction between the freedom of difference and the non-indifference of responsibility, or, more specifically, between the social-contract of a free-market "global democracy" and the much more literal vocation of asymmetrical solicitude in a dying world. For our silence throughout an age wherein all but the most exorbitant forms of responsibility are without effect, only a dialogue beyond even the seemingly authentic labor of a "being-with," or rather, beyond all laboring for an authenticity in Heidegger's *mitsein*, is not a refrain.

The Passion

> The second shedding of the blood of Jesus most sweet which gave the rose of the passion its crimson color, consists in the sweat of blood of Christ praying in agony.

> —Bonaventura (trans. from *Vitis Mystica*)

Therefore, let your love lead your steps to Jesus wounded . . . Not only *see in His hands the print of the nails*, with the apostle Thomas, not only put your finger into the place of the nails, not only put your hand into His side, but enter with your whole being through the door of His side into Jesus' heart itself.

—Bonaventura (trans. from *De perfectione vitae ad sorores*)

It may be said that the vanishing point of the panels of blood and ash in the Rothko Chapel, and in its poem at Taggart's constant urging, is inscription, and that these panels, themselves the depths we were to surpass by monumentalizing language (but by proving true to them as groom and bride), attend, if not to life, then like a funeral for peace avert our lives and mourn for victims of the highest price: the unending betrayal of Christ. It is especially in, or according to, the movement of the line that Taggart, in an almost wholly inexplicit sense, effects—rather than establishes—an anamnesis of the indigence at Calvary. Never has a poem struck me so personally, though I realize that my sense of its relation, or even its resemblance, to the Passion of Christ is by no means unquestionable. Nevertheless, what I perceive as the contour of an absolution of the language—as in a mirror to my own obsession with the death and the second coming of the messiah—may simply be a sense in which, after Bonaventura's injunction, the structure of the poem is also that of the heart of Christ. Thus having faced the expectations of "The Rothko Chapel Poem," perhaps as the Israelites in the wilderness did the flames of revelation in the face of Moses—through a veil of mercy, I have been unable to fully countenance the sorrow I perceive within the poem without a measure, however extreme, of contextualization in terms of the late medieval and Renaissance traditions of Passion mysticism.

If a formation peaks, and riddles silence, space and time without this consequence: *that we must grieve to be survived*, then it must also be said that this reinscription of the beginning-not-to-be itself—traducing form with flow—does not appease. With this defeat of the senses in spite of repetition, with this re-petitioning of dispensation—that, if only to give us away as the bride to immediacy, we let the measure bay, and bring down sentencing and terror to the seed from which all hierarchs progress. Let it be said that this giving way to a shape, this giving shape to a cry from the depths has been reached only by way of an asymmetry, perhaps a psalmistry, of what is other over what is the same—an asymmetry paralleling and in due time undertaking through human renewal the movement upward of our always over-extended horizons off the vertical allowing life.

The confusion of our movement between that in which silence is harbored, and that which is a burgeoning of nothingness, manifests itself as repetition in this poem. But always only *as if* language surpasses us, that which is actually infinite *passes itself* where we happen to meet: as we speak at a loss it is passed onto bone, and is the bottom notch; it is passed on the Cross; it is passed from the fire atop a pyre to the line of fire. For Taggart the way may be known only through what in all our endeavors is given-way to according to poetry: among what corridors in all our encounters, and what arches under our inscrutability at once, and undeniably, give way onto wanton exchange. The way of following the example of poetry may be known only in keeping with, or rather only in preparation for this being-in-keeping-with, the vision without which even our hindsight destroys us.

Taggart is concerned to account for encounter considered as vision; not necessarily lacking for metaphor, but beyond manipulation in auditions of invisibility, the vision now hidden by, now distant from insight and so much more glaring than any error as understood upon reflection, stands in this manner of speaking as a sign of the offering of signs. The thrilling oxymoron or paradox of auditory vision is itself a sign. The poet of vision makes of him or herself a point of reference for the paradox of signs to seek; an anchor for annihilation at this time, the poet of vision neither holds it off nor plunges through it, but is receptive and most certainly exposed, retaining contraries until, in the throes of composition, the "not quite parallel lines"—of Father and child, of the thee and the I—cross the cut on it enough to sever the tongue, that it might now be loosed. The regression of signification in mediacy is inhibited by the poet of vision. Poetry of vision consigns the poet to being invisible as a sign of the offering of signs before our eyes, to being assigned as an eroded face unmoored among the cogs of dialectic and reflection, but tending toward prominence among the senses now at large and shared by all. Lacking vision, we refuse to deny our identity, though we will of course struggle to hide it in the unlikely event of Judgment Day. We do not admit that reflection too extends to the sleepless many yet to come this flaw we so casually sow, but the same unleashing of nightmares that we ourselves awoke to and employed in giving way to mirror images portends no pause, for we are only under fire when it falls.

"The Rothko Chapel Poem," like the title poem of *Peace on Earth*, is among the most significant works of art created in the United States since the Second World War; in this it must be considered as definitively complementary to the Rothko paintings themselves. Truly it is a poem of our climate as Stevens conceived this relation. One is tempted, following Duncan's marvelous introduction to Taggart's *Dodeka*, to imagine in-tact numerological and geometrical patterns at work as the poem unfolds. Pages often inversely mirror each other, sometimes creating a kind of Jacob's ladder circuitry by which all that comes down must go up to survive, sometimes playing a shell game of phrase rearrangement with the horizontal axes, with the structure of the line. I have sought in vain to find a geometry that the movements of mirroring and inversion, so akin to what Howe sometimes does, might attain-to in extending the boundaries of transparency at the level of the line; now, however, I must relinquish my search to the simple recognition of the emergence of shape from these pages of lines, like a gathering—a standing wave—of transitivity, a mindfulness of repetition meant to be analogous to the development of seams and emphases in Rothko's color-field process of "saturation," which Taggart describes as follows, as if describing his own poem, in "Eight Headnotes":

> The important thing is that the entire
> painting at the center of the triptych
> contains several smaller Rothko's within
> itself and creates, in the process, several
> cross shapes through the coming together
> of horizontal and vertical forms. This
> means that our attention is always
> engaged, caught, by each portion of the
> central painting and as a whole. It is,
> indeed, a center from which there can be
> "slippage" as the eye travels, but no
> evasion.[15]

Considering as well, then, the major transformation through which Taggart's work once went, as manifested in the arrival of *Peace on Earth* after years of apprenticeship to the perfectionist Objectivism of Zukofsky, an apprenticeship in prosodic construction going beyond even Zukofsky's with the meta-patternings developed in *Dodeka*: considering, that is, the radical departure from Objectivism for which *Peace on Earth* is like a fiery point of embarcation in this poet's search for soul (in Coltrane, Rothko, Hopper, Eckhart, Marvin Gaye, Melville, Emily Dickinson, Duncan, Howe, Messiaen, etc.), we cannot fail to conclude that no, precision is not the motive of the ghost that feeds these patterns such a poem. Rather than objectification, something more akin to assignation is at work, and the petitioning implied by repetition here, being already heteronomous, already given

---

[15] John Taggart, *Loop* (Sun and Moon Press: Los Angeles, 1991) p. 131. [hereafter cited in text as L]

way to in a ban on-high, and made of pain, like Abraham's consistent "here I am," is as a scourge to composition that exacts a kind of path among the eaves of ash, the burning canopy of Southeast Asia and of Eden's tree, the outer reaches under fire from the setting Sun, or in a beam between the lines that slip outside of space, but give a shape to time and strike the waiting bud. Just as Howe, to reach the Tomb where she will prophesy, must follow Mary through the night and not receive the Sun, now we must follow the blood of Jesus through the space upon his side, the wound we owe our blood until the flow runs dry. Little did I know of where the poet was, from whence he came or where she sought to go, until the journey undertaken here became a paradox, and Kierkegaardian by any means. After Barth and Weil, no one until Taggart has given way to Kierkegaard with the decisiveness necessary to be true to the entire range of paradoxicality that thrives within his thought. One is justified, I think, in coming away from Taggart's work—and its engagement with Kierkegaard—with the impression that the bulk of post-structuralism may in fact be but a grand preliminary to the hermeneutic engagement that *Fear and Trembling* still awaits. Whereas Marx's revolutionary teleology contains within itself the seeds of factory built totalitarianism, Kierkegaard's encompassing religiosity in *Fear and Trembling* sustains a pitch of paradox that, if followed openly, would lead to potlatch in a social sphere abandoned by Enlightenment to reflection and bureaucracy. Taking a cue from Kierkegaard's ontological definition of repetition ("Repetition and recollection are the same movement, except in opposite directions, for what is recollected has been, is repeated backward, whereas genuine repetition is recollected forward."[16]), Taggart manifests not simply a poetics of, but a physically dependent, ill-advisedly replenished laboring of the Kierkegaardian onto-theology, though he

[16] Soren Kierkegaard, *Fear and Trembling/Repetition*, Trans. Howard V. Hong and Edna H. Hong (Princeton Univ. Press: New Jersey, 1983), p. 131. [hereafter cited in text as FT/R]

does so less in a consent to repetition than in the repetition of a decision. Long before and after he begins to repeat himself in *Peace on Earth*, with words that lead to *Loop*, Taggart *decides*, and does not hide from the fire of God that will fall. Though repetition adapts the poet's eyes to vision, to the voices of life—of a child in pain—his face under fire from on-high is sacrificed. See the poem "Not Quite Parallel Lines":

back to the wave and to the question of position

the wave may become a blade broad as the horizon itself

or it may become narrow with a sharp point wrapped in fire

whether horizon or wrapped point the question remains

(L 184)

. . . or the poem "The Reading of Something Written (2)":

To be invaded by sound interiors invaded

invaded by the sound of word and child

having to hear the voice through a speaker

having been invaded having to hear the voice

having been invaded having to go on hearing.

Ourselves letting ourselves nothing less

ourselves letting ourselves be gathered

gathered by word and child for the voice

the voice lays one the voice lays another

lays one interior lays another the same

letting ourselves lie together before

letting and lying gathered by a speaker

hearing occurs in us because of a speaker

hearing in us has to be a kind of mishearing.
(L 195)

In "The Rothko Chapel Poem," Taggart takes us even further toward a receptivity to influx, to a reversed asymmetry between immanence and the outside, and in doing so almost in terms of the Dantean conceit of the journey from Hell to Heaven, without getting out of Hell he arduously plays-out what he sees not as the possibility of a leap between, but as an opposition between the leaps of, the two movements that Kierkegaard in *Fear and Trembling* names the movements of resignation and faith. In the paradox of faith, when only impossibility is manifested, in fact infinite possibility is affirmed because with God all things are possible. The author of *Fear and Trembling* cannot compare his mere *understanding* of this paradox to Abraham's *embrace* of it as manifested in his raising of a knife heteronomously over Isaac in the Holy Land. Like Johannes de Silentio as a "poet-dialectician," Taggart as a Kierkegaardian poet is aware of the limits, not of what he is proposing, but of what can happen once he does so. But rather than attach himself to limits of any kind, imagining more, he exhorts us to replenish these limits, to dispense with all resistance in the midst of—in the lack of continuity between—infinite resignation and the leap of faith; on the margins of our sacrifice to life, we must be prepared to understand by "resignation," then, something at the same time productive of and yet entirely opposed to isolation:

I am wandering again within this room

I am not making a move toward ladders

73

from those rooms into this black room

away from the weddings wedding rooms

seething and writhing within this room

echoes of one scream within itself

screaming within that will not decay

this is a different kind of domination

from those rooms into this black room

I have moved away all the way away

I have made the movement of resignation

I have performed the first movement

away from the weddings wedding rooms.
(L 168)

Though "only when the individual has emptied himself in the infinite . . . has the point been reached where faith can break through" (FT/R p. 69), away from the wedding rooms, from the Biblical figure of sacred espousal—election and covenant being the nuptials by which the human and God become bound—what befalls the poet can only be described as a kind of banishment from all atemporality: "As soon as I want to begin, everything reverses itself, and I take refuge in the pain of resignation. I am able to swim in life, but I am too heavy for this mystical hovering. To exist in such a way that my contrast to existence constantly expresses itself as the most beautiful and secure harmony with it—this I cannot do."(FT/R 50) Like Johannes de Silentio, Taggart has no faith. In the "room where the second movement is to be made // movement of rosy transparency the self rosy // self relating to self willing to be itself", the poet speaks, but says, "I am in this room I do not make the movement // don't complete movement I'm the child of pain"(L 169). Taggart is, like Kierkegaard in the bulk of his writings, unable to make the movement that he nevertheless recognizes as the highest—as described by Kierkegaard in terms of an assumption of the self into transparency, in godliness by virtue of an embracement of the irrecuperable, which entails, as a leap, a releasement of relation itself from all symmetry. Perhaps Kierkegaard is extending a more precise invitation to what, in Plato's *Phaedrus*, looms vaguely over even the realm of Ideas as divine madness. The exceeded-to, rather than regressed-to, "child of pain," in part being incapable of election, but also, ultimately, refusing the possibility of it in the "weddings wedding rooms," remains alone in the refuge of pain. The "child of pain" of the poet's refusal of election is accompanied by the guilt of the poet's being imposed upon by his own painful sorrowlessness, by the clarity through which what is sorrowful is finally seen, but is incendiary only to a feeling of pain as the remaining mode of continuity between the witnesses to and the victims of our crimes, in a world in which children are sorrowful *and* in pain:

> The child is not sufficiently reflective to feel pain, and yet his sorrow is infinitely deep. He is not sufficiently reflective to have an idea of sin and guilt; when he sees an adult suffer, it does not cross his mind to think about that, and yet if the reason for the suffering is hidden from him, there is a dark presentiment of the reason in the child's sorrow . . . On the other hand, when an adult sees a young person, a child, suffer, the pain is greater, the sorrow less. The more pronounced the idea of guilt, the greater the pain, the less profound the sorrow. [17]

[17] Soren Kierkegaard, *Either/Or* pt. 1., trans. Edward V. Hong and Edna H. Hong (Princeton Univ. Press: New Jersey, 1987), p. 148.

The paradox of taking refuge in pain, of the non-immanent irreplaceability of the individual called before God or the face of the other, though perhaps a vestige of the purest forms of prophetic Judeo-Christianity *and* Romanticism, nevertheless echoes irrepressibly in the post-Holocaust contexts of Levinas's enslavement of subjectivity to the call of the coronated other, Weil's experience of affliction as faith, Howe's "true submission and subjection" to the Word, and Taggart's "this is a different kind of domination."

If, according to "Return to Dehiscence," "there's no releasement into the arms of a loving father / releasement's into the desert without distinction," and if the wilderness of Exodus stood on all sides of, and in the midst of those who entered it as if to mark for them, from now until the end of time, the "bridal time" of God, then we must assume that the bride has been stopped, not by the decree or the demise of God, but by the isolation of the desert from our chosen path—the path whereon self-mastery has trod, destroying faith. We did not walk the line that disappears. "The Rothko Chapel Poem" provides a kind of blind alley into and out of the bridal time. The poet in the rooms of the groom and bride becomes blind to distinctions between rouge and blood, between ash and the back of his hand, between transparency and the lack of blood; but when the blindnesses as such are opened up—with prominence given to what may, in turn, be heard should someone scream—the structures of reception, having merged, begin to ripen for a fall.

Taggart engages language in a struggle of and with abysmal welcomings of the spirit, rhythm foundering and made nameless in a world in which will and spirit meet but cannot speak and merge. Because in consequence our silence contradicts all unity in principle, the fault-line laid—our logic placed—where will and spirit fail to meet must banish peace from every dialogue, and words from all but war, but it maintains the pace of sophistry, of which a "miracle" or two have since been told. Taggart tells us, no, there is no sophistry for war: but never less than there are words, then there is war to fear, and therefore still a loss of language that must come to bear.

from Kierkegaard's notebooks:

> In the sphere of freedom, the word "mediation" has again done damage, because, coming from logic, it helped to make the transcendence of movement illusory. In order to prevent this error or this dubious compromise between the logical and freedom, I have thought that "repetition" could be used in the sphere of freedom.
>
> If it gets the right to rule, then freedom disperses itself and is never in a position to realize repetition. Then freedom despairs of itself but still never forgets repetition. But in the moment of despair a change takes place with regard to repetition, and freedom takes on a religious expression, by which repetition appears as atonement, which is repetition sensu eminentiori and something different from mediation, which always merely describes the nodal points of oscillation in the progress of immanence.
>
> If one wishes to illustrate that the meaning of repetition in the world of the individuality is different from its meaning in the world of nature and in a simple repetition, I do not think one can do it more definitely. When repetition is defined in that way, it is: transcendent, a religious movement by virtue of the absurd—when the borderline of the wondrous is reached, eternity is the true repetition.
>
> (FT/R 308, 320, 305 resp.)

Taggart as well is concerned to choose eternity over immanence in the battle of termini over the movement and mediacy of a fallen world. In his poems he might be said to emphasize that insofar as the absurd effect of repetition is to atone for the mere "oscillation" of immanence (the dialectic of identity) in a movement of absolution (as opposed to an absolutizing movement), only when it is induced from without (by the absurd) is repetition effective against, rather than reifying of, the organizing principles of our ruin. Revolution entails not just a usurpation of forces at the scene of oppression, but a deathblow delivered to the moment in the movement of those forces that is specifically designed to at all times reproduce the conditions amenable to that movement as it sets the scene: the moment of awakening at which the poetic deathblow, that of repetition (the very opposite of, and the true offense to, reproduction), is directed is in our possession as self-reflexivity. In "Were You / Notes & A Poem For Michael Palmer," Taggart brings to mind the case of gospel singing in being faced with so limited a set of criteria for response and engagement as that which the dominant discourses, both academic and poetic, on the left afford us as writers today. But so complex are the paradoxes sustaining the idea that repetition is movement, and the idea that movement is absurd, that we can hardly take a breath between the lines he writes without being consumed with the guilt of our own already inaudible voice. In poetry such as this the instauration in the line runs as a duct to immanence; Captain Ahab, for instance, is not just caught by his own line, but he is alive in *these* lines: his desire is never so real as when he dies, but it enters the rest of the world when it's real. Taggart composes his poems as a challenger not *of* the limits of form, but *for* the victims of innovation. The alterity so dominant in, and over, writing in the 19th century, and still at work in the poetry of Stevens and Riding, Spicer, Taggart and Howe, seems to have completely vanished from recent poetry—distinctly on a parallel course, it seems, with the process by which, since Kierkegaard came into French, the idea of irrecuperable alterity has been minted for the theoretical economy, and is now presided over as a precondition for the practice of *différance*. I have the sense that the remarkable changes that have taken place at the level of hermeneutics after structuralism have brought, as well, a drastic end to the possibility, so prominent in Benjamin, of a redemption from without—requiring a radical shift in consciousness, in a no less material than messianic sense. An end brought by discourse to the suprahierarchical is in fact symptomatic of the process by which, at the level of culture, mediacy itself has been deified. One might come to question recent trends in critical theory on the basis of a sense of the fact that the other, and I mean the other person, cannot be considered as absolute, in poetry or elsewhere, without connotations of a kind of idolatrous fetishization or coinage. Hence it has become necessary to understand the "you" in the work of a poet like Paul Celan in a completely historical sense. But among the avant-garde poets who work in theory today, the untrammeled denial of address to the other—the heteronomous call to responsibility being as distinct from materiality as dialogue is from anonymity—is simply indefensible, but definitively symptomatic of the final stage of the absorption of the entire possibility of signs into the drift of anonymity, the very fount of global capitalism.

By virtue of the coupling of an absolutization of response with the decision of absolution—with the face-eating epiphany of the voice from the whirlwind in Job—the act of composition in Taggart's work in some way partakes, perhaps, in the rarely modern, if only in the case of Weil, tradition of indiscernible martyrdom as depicted in Second Isaiah. Taggart's is a radically traditional response. To the same extent that the Will to Power overarches those others whose calls it elicits and resounds within, until it trods them down, the power of spirit conforms those who are called to it on the other's account by a higher voice. He who is other to those who are other to him is conformed by alterity, while those who are other to him are enthroned. Precipitated not simply vicariously—by means of an idea of dissolution or infusion—but in being suffused with a holy voice that, like

the scapegoat, lows long after all the flesh is gone: "our
attention is drawn toward or by a quality of aware sacrifice,
aware restriction." (L 210)

> When we turn from the poem, what we
> have to feel is the falling away, the utter
> lack of its clarity all around us.
>
> (L 213)

PUT IT ALL ON THE ALTAR

"Liberty" too is a demand of the anti-poetic.

—Robert Duncan (from
The H.D. Book, 1961)

Lost is the illegibility of a universe, a universe the limitlessness of which is a resistance to ascent, but to the revelatory a sieve; the limitless is but a permutation of the face of God. Lost with the language of God is the illegibility of descent in those who live, that they might gather irresistibly in what the language gives. Lost though it may be to internecine legibility—and to a war between the Cosmos and the Occident—the exteriority of a human, all too human universe may still exist: but as a language of the loss as such, considered as a call for which this language is, as prophecy, the unresolved sensorium that comes across. What we might experience, that is, in encountering the death of God, beyond all license, is simply a moment at which loss as such is infused with the power of being a call. With the death of God—and both Nietzsche and Dostoyevsky knew this—not only is everything permitted, but prophecy is by definition resurrected. If God did not die of natural causes, as the Deists once thought, of what was the death of God a consequence: suicide or murder? With what except, on the one hand, mysticism, on the other, prophecy, do we respond, respectively, to the suicide or murder of a God? Certain sages have said that everything must be permitted before the Messiah will enter. Within Judaism there were once entire sects—especially the radical wing of the 17th century Sabbatians—devoted to outbursts of sin, which were proliferated as a goad—of holy lawlessness—to the post-messianic *tikkun*. To add to this the foment of an utter rectitude that is nevertheless in complete accord with lawlessness, I have said that there is urgency in an enunciation the existence of which is, with respect to the impossibility of what is announced, necessarily deviant. Embodied as urgency in such an enunciation, what I have also called prophecy is thus enacted as a transposition of the word—from the paradox of, to utter deviance from, impossibility which does not, therefore, continue to be realized as such.

For Robert Duncan

On the basis of a profound distrust of instrumental
models of language, and in coincidence with the entrench-
ment of such models in the university-centered mainstream
poetry renaissance of the seventies, remarkable strides—of
theoretical resistance to, and aesthetic liberty from, the
mainstream sensibility—have been taken by avant-garde
poets during the last twenty years. Yet, as is the case with all
bourgeois transformations, the moment of discovery—of
the discovery of resistance—has passed. When the tenets of
resistance become presumptions, they necessarily
overdetermine that resistance, with the consequence of one-
dimensionality at the level of practice.

I will provisionally characterize an emerging resistance to
current trends in the literary avant-garde as a "provocation
in the face of an ossified focus on the signifier"—as I worded
it in a recent letter to Charles Bernstein. All too predictably
in opposition to, and in evasion of, or even disempowerment
of, alterity—situated now at the level of content and the non-
symbolic—do our meta-linguistic formulae, methods, and
relativisms gather as poetry in the midst of what might well
be but a vast and irreversible capitulation to capitalist
strategy and scientism on the part of our most socio-centric
poets. "Process" is upheld over "closure," but to avoid and
deny all attempts at a departure further from closure than
any process is, one must neglect to take into account the fact
that capitalism is the only process: we resist bringing subjec-
tion of any kind to a close in immediacy, but we must lapse
as in submission to a cataclysmic equity. In a moment of
despair I would characterize what is at this point required of
the avant-garde, then, as a vast expiation—involving years
of completely re-oriented study and practice—for its be-
trayal of the radical historical traditions of the sacred and the
creative word. Just as Duncan has so brilliantly described
and constellated certain of these traditions in the *H.D. Book*,
Susan Howe, having brought a truly covenantal power into
the language of romance and revelation as Duncan knew it,

also bears the heterodox forth from principles of form into a condition of historic prophecy. Under the tremendous weight of a history of rupture and expectation waged against the Church and State by prophets and mystics in the heterodox spiritual tradition, both Howe and Taggart invite a destruction of power by fire and the face of God, although a release into absolute love is not wholly denied by the call to which power conforms in the language they've heard. Again judging the state of poetry in terms of the recent arrival of *Loop* and *The Nonconformist's Memorial* into print, I am forced to conclude that, if only in the work of these two poets, the post-Vietnam avant-garde of poetry in the USA has come still farther, finally, than ever toward the goal of responsibility as Duncan understood it: as a desire told to those who write, for poetry, that is, to finally reckon with itself not only in terms of its claims to innovation at the urging of theory—claims which in our day amount to a self-distancing from convention through structuralist critique, and a stance of irony towards the authorial position and the possibility of reception on the part of the reader—but more importantly, and for the first time in perhaps 40 years (since Olson's *In Cold Hell, In Thicket*) in terms of the iniquity of history in the West since the Homeric epics, with its movement toward rationalization and enlightenment as Weber and Adorno, respectively, understood these terms.

Always beginning radically with the universality of language understood as a ruin, the poem in the hands of both Taggart and Howe tends indirectly, though not indecisively, toward an ecstasy set-up against restraints of immanence, and against the violence of totalities without restraint. Tending toward ecstasy to reach the claims of the outside of language—of sound in the claims of the child, of Leviathan, of the prophetess bound at the stake, of the night-sky and the Sun's end, of the spirit and in witness, in the fire and the sign's role in rounds sung outside space and time, and in mercy, in pity and peace, and the life-force of rime—poetry in attending to ecstasy of any kind thus draws toward itself that possibility of law-destroying violence, an onset of sacrifice in what we would otherwise and even mystically draw toward on the basis of need. With the onset of unintentional desire, centricity and symmetry recede: the falling fire of the other on the converted eye is now belief. I heard a preacher urging his parishioners to be as prophets in the fight against perennial hardship; because Elijah "put it all on the altar," he said, "the fire of God did fall." Peace may be maintained in a spirit of relativism, but not at the expense of the prophetic in a war for equality.

Contrary to the reigning oppositional ideology in contemporary poetry, the altar on which we lay our writings down is not of language, but language is itself the sacrifice: we must indeed lay it on the altar of the other person. Not the altar of language—but, of the other, the altar on which it is sacrificed is the milestone poetry seeks. Only in a radicalized, not subverted, transparency do the dying embers of the contextual get fanned. A blaze is then fed what we've hidden and that which still stands. Poets are on the road to Emmaus, but all recognition of the other on this road is poetry. Mary was urged to speak, and to console even as she wept disconsolately. Her urges unearthed Him. What remains of Mary the Mother of the Incarnate Word is poetry: the anointer of a word that resurrects. What remains is a subject speaking solely insofar as what is said is received, or is encountered insofar as what is saved is unseen.

To the degree to which it is epistemologically presupposed, the "systematicity of language" is nothing other, though more fatal, than a stand-in for what is actually the systematicity of our own denial of the claims of language at the level of the other's unsystematizable cry, pain and weeping being our one still legitimate refrain, what is most human, that is, in a linguisitic system that passes between us only a seemingly endless proliferation of soliloquies of domination, and an intersubjectvity founded on and hounded by all narcissism, corporately generated, and maddeningly fallacious as the consequence of a concocted lack. We are trapped in an interplay vested with strife at the level of what are by now our almost platonically inalienable rights of ownership, which fuel the withering dissemination of universal captialism in a world without outlet for universality at the level of sacrifice. We are denying the claims, that is, of exteriority itself, of Levinas's *otherwise than being*, on the writing process and on the position in society from which, in heeding what is otherwise than that by which its instrument—language—is always manipulated rather than given, poetry severs itself, not in the explosion of codes, but in an offering passed over itself by means of a deduction of symmetry from the wager of content, in a risk reducing to ashes all sense of the center, and, under the lash of transcendence and song, reducing subjection itself now unmasked as the quest for which mediation in the West has been the false-front of merely market-driven symmetry, mythologically immobilized as "liberty" in the bourgeois catalogue of progress past the possibility of sacrifice. Howe and Taggart insist, that is, that in this life and not in any way in spite of all claims, language being only one among the many claims, some as yet unrealized, on our attention: in spite, that is, of the barrier of language, or of the tendency to merely revel in its availability, writing functions not in the process of capitulation to a cultural void, not, that is, in language as a mirror held up to division and absence, compounding the forces which keep us apart, but rather, and indeed more precisely, in a final resistance to these forces, to all that, including critique, keeps the people from taking the stage as a chorus of the gloriously redeemed. This is a gospel resistance that keeps us together in the off-stage of the outside—the threat to all theater in the understudy's cry—or under wings not ever spent by winds, but spread before us as though through a force of verisimilitude to Benjamin's Angel's vision—depicting as it does the process of history as a wind that, under the shelter of progress, blows between paradise and annihilation. In the wings from which such a stage, the stage of symbolic order, might be spied and rightly sacrificed in the face to face relation that the very fact of language gives a name—a fact that only poetry corroborates—language is itself understood to have a meaning,

meaning being determined from without even though the possibility of meaning presupposes language.

John Taggart's refusal of the "second movement," Susan Howe's breakout into "perfect primeval Consent," rise perhaps in tandem to the few occasions of our innocence of what we've done to this world with words. With implications in a mystical tradition of which he was only incidentally aware, in the *Tractatus* Wittgenstein offers the following injunction: *whereof one cannot speak, thereof one must be silent*. Like Heidegger—and this is what makes the presumed contradiction between them an identification as well—Wittgenstein plunders the idea of silence for a counterpoise to positivism. We will return endlessly to the question of whether the logocentricity to which we are limited by reason *precludes the actuality of*, or actually *posits the transcendence of*, that which exceeds it in the name of God. It is within these terms that radical skepticism as characterized earlier in this essay, and the limited skepticism of the Enlightenment critique of theocentricity—the very bastion of human self-deification through modernization—stand in dialogue. It is not, however, through our *listening* to that before which we fall silent that we fall back on reason accordingly (according to a near-misreading of Wittgenstein's injunction), but it is through our failure to heed our recognition of it that, like Wittgenstein, we master silence. It is, to put it another way, in the effects of our failure to listen at all that reason invests itself and gains a ground. The step beyond a recognition of silence to a silencing of reason is one that both Wittgenstein and Heidegger placed before themselves: Wittgenstein refused to take the step, while Heidegger, with his fellow Germans, of course mistook it. That to which we listen when we fall silent is not what we fall silent before, but what comes before us when it falls. For the moment I must stress that it is toward an other at risk, then, and not toward alterity itself, which is at large, that one must turn an ear prophetically and risk defeat.

Iconomachia

> This is the masterpiece of a modern politician, how to qualifie, and mould the sufferance and subjection of the people to the length of that foot that is to tread on their necks, how rapine may serve it selfe with the fair, and honourable pretences of publick good, how the puny Law may be brought under the wardship, and controul of lust, and will, in which attempt if they fall short, then must a superficial colour of reputation by all means direct or indirect be gotten to wash over the unsightly bruse of honor. To make men governable in this manner their precepts mainly tend to break a nationall spirit, and courage by count'nancing open riot, luxury, and ignorance, till having thus disfigur'd and made men beneath men, as *Juno* in the Fable of *Io*, they deliver up the poor transformed heifer of the Commonwealth to be stung and vext with the breese, and goad of oppression under the custody of some *Argus* with a hundred eyes of jealousie.

> —John Milton (from *Of Reformation*, 1641)

If humanity is knower in the same language in which God is creator, then the language at our disposal is in fact the very degradation of what, as far as bodies go, we really are in being given ground. Far from being that which distinguishes us from animals, language is that which degrades us in their eyes, for by "their eyes" I mean the eyes are watching God. Notwithstanding the political correctness of the rejection of the Pauline spirit/letter dualism, the time has come for us to flush from the thickets of post-Modern formalist anti-transcendentalism the lame-duck theology still underlying

it: language was once the barrier to God, but now poetry is
our monument to Language. Language *is* a barrier, the
barrier beyond which only our victims speak on, but in
speaking bequeath to our hindsight and foresight the mean-
ing of language itself and the promise of life. But now poetry
is our promise to a Language the limitlessness of which bars
exteriority in order to effect a kind of catalystness, a lock-
and-key on influx and heat—this avant-gardist posture of
distance from "convention" being the merely formal barrier
to receptivity, but a barrier that, in eliminating expiation,
becomes a universe through the worship of means. As
always, but never more perilously so than now, we are faced
with the struggle of overcoming institutional reservations
toward, and epsitemological mediations of our passion—be
they in the form of self-prioritizing commentary or theoreti-
cal poetry at this time. I am steadfast in my misgivings about
merely critical discourse: no matter where it stands politi-
cally, critique will always take as its primary, though
unadmitted-to goal, the continued introduction of condi-
tions most conducive to its remaining supreme in the order
of cultural production as designed by Arnold in the nine-
teenth century, with all the requisite denial of extremity and
inspiration that its institutionality, and its prestigious place
within the institution, presuppose. I am undoubtedly out-
dated in upholding the primary/secondary, poetry/commen-
tary dichotomy by saying that theory is to poetry what the
church is to spirit: the church of theory keeps poetry from
finding its own way to where it is justified before we even
speak, to where it is heard, which is in the streets with a
vengeance and, as Melville once said, in the same way that
God would take to the streets were the word God not in the
dictionary. Were poetry not morassed within the university,
radicalism would not be limited to poetics. We must em-
battle the very clarity with which the call for justice is itself
called to order in terms of professional norms. Institutionality,
of which the university is only the most ironically, or the least
positivistically devoted source, is the seat of iniquity. If,
following post-structuralist psychoanalytic theory, we claim
that the language of maternity is pre-symbolic, and the

language of the Father is symbolic, then it is theory itself, the hyper-symbolic, rather than the language of the Father, of meaning and socialization, that keeps poetry from ushering in—over the clamor of computer keyboards in a world turning into America—the voices of a post-symbolic age.

"Language itself," and the "autonomy" of Language, in already being the basis of two generations of avant-garde poetry since the 70's, are never anything more than ideas (and suspiciously socio-economically determined ideas at that) except in the effects of our use of language as determined by them when they become presumptions: effects which for our purposes may be categorized as denials of address. Language under this idea of it is an agent of indifference that models itself on a theoretical quest for process. We must aspire not to extend the horizons of language, and hence dissipate the possibility of face to face dialogue as distinct from on-line spontaneity, but to be in effect over-extended toward the other person's command of our language, which is simultaneously within language and yet dependent on a sense in which this language meets its end. That is, a radically transparent language—of an address to the other—is not in the confines of *itself*, to say the least; it is confined from the beginning by an other. Language is not constitutive, nor is what it operates within circumscribed by it. Indeed what language is always within is simply striking-distance—of the divergence between availability and excess, difference and non-indifference, form and address. In fact a radicalization of transparency admits of no refusal of paradox and no rehearsal of terms in our overcoming of self-sufficiency. We must labor, then, not to get in touch with the liminal anonymity of language—with the process by which, as a barrier to conscience, it survives—but to, in our use of language, reduce ourselves to a point of access further from closure than any process, in a redistribution through, and a final exposure to, asymmetry of other over self as the only dialogue.

We must prepare ourselves for an offering requiring of us not just the whole of what we are, including language, but the very fact that we *are* in the first place. Going beyond even Heidegger's quest for the difference of Being from beings, we must pose to ourselves the question of what, in the other person's face, by the decree of countenance, the *otherwise than being* raises against our very right to be. Perhaps the face of the other may be glimpsed only in masochism. Under the equally dire threats of neo-conservativism in our culture and the increasing academicization of our liberalism, by poetry we must mean that there is always more time for anarchy to perhaps render with us a part in some hitherto repressed, but still dissenting harmony, than there is time for ivory-tower irony, however keen its analysis may be, to take effect against the policies of a status quo from which nothing can distinguish itself merely by being distant from it. In our monumentalization of deferment we have sought to self-consciously evacuate, rather than laboriously reclaim, the mechanism of meaning, only to avoid and therefore void community in being ideologically systematic in our use of deferment as a method and not a conversion. Deferment in its current usage variously renders spite and play upon the page, and the "community" it affords, in being molded more by the demands of theory than by the possibility of con-science, puts on hold all calls except the most generous of those coming in from the university. Howe and Taggart rise to this sordid occasion and obligate us to its downfall at the expense of our merely textual resistance to authority. Demands at the expense of our own authority over the process of writing are made on us, yet without the requisite indiffer-ence to the sacred authority of the other person—in these poems the victims of history—over irony and avant-gardism. While writing of this kind revolts from all defenses against responsibility, in doing so the challenge risen-to in fact demonstrates that it remains to be seen if a world redeemed is not in any case necessarily contended in speech rather than dissembled in writing, writing being less a condition for history than indelibly symptomatic of it, or rather, more a foothold for our part—the only self-conscious part—in the verdict of this history with which inscription coincides and engages our silence, than a stepping-stone between the banks of the masses and the ruling class.

The final reference of writing is a silence filled by face to face encounters surpassing language and inviting sustenance. Victorious over closure as we are today, we necessarily remain unable to close ourselves off from desirelessness. We have yet to totalize solicitude. Only in surpassing language *in* our relations, rather than *and* our relations—the difference here being none other than that between redemption and transcendence—are we bound to what is outside, without being capable of opposing it in turn to reap identity. Speech is a symptom of the silence that the very possibility of writing produces, writing being the artificer not of tragic proportions, but of a refusal to overcome our self-sufficiency as tragedians. Even the writings of the scriptural prophets were in large part transcriptions of publicly delivered speeches and outcries. Had writing never been a possibility language would never have dislodged itself from the senses to fill warning cries that, less than surpassing instinct, foreshadowed by its repression as such our self-destruction as the species that writes. Simply put, because we do not know of the need for a narrowing of choices, because we are forced to consume, and because we have chosen, as property- and copyright-owners, award-winners, chair-holders etc., to presume that we must be conscious of fulfillment for there to be fulfillment, we do not have the ability to distinguish, from the monotony of consciousness, the stirrings of conscience that would gather in us as a surge of redistribution, as a sacrifice on the order of the infinite, uninhibitable in accord with an historical devastation the proportions of which are as timeless in their structural continuity as they are vast in their material implications for the proletariat.

The sole purpose of the total influence of corporate interests over the human condition, over our privacy *and* our very definition of community by way of mass-media, is of course to diverge from the superstructure of the world—the abode of history—the stirrings of conscience that all dimensions of the human harbor and that they must one day actually be if life is to in any ethical sense go on. Yet the relative insuffuciency of poetry has less to do with its cultural marginality *per se* than with the odious marginalization of the humanities in the public academy, where funding for cultural outreach and advocacy is reserved disproportionately for athletics. We can continue to legitimately point to a history of literary discourse in which the various radicalisms of poetry—no longer even decried as specters, but found in a similar position to Communism and in fact to eschatology of any kind in the New World Order—would appear to us as nothing more than a heap of paradigmatically non-differentiated fodder for our own Foucauldian critiques of normalization.

As much out of our hands as are the answers to them are the questions of which only poets are aware. But why, why is our radical poetry suddenly so superior to passion, so self-consciously disaffected that, in the blink of an eye, in the sweep, say, of Elvin Jones's coming in on a periphery of the wind thirty seconds into *A Love Supreme*—that in the moment of *this* decision, whereby pose is the throe, but the horn is exposure itself, and the sound, be it spoken in tongues or else blown at the Sun, heralds love toward us all: spirit in the music of a love supreme reveals all critique of spirit, literary post-Modernism's fundament and livelihood, to be the denial that it is, as violent toward as it is gamesome with the demands of address and extremity, with the plain fact of our crying out for the response that the very presence of language presupposes and feeds, a response coming only from the prophets and those few like Blake and Dickinson, Taggart and Howe, with whom we'd open wide the mantle on which we have built, if only unsteadily in terms of the distance our steps must now sate, or in terms of the sky toward which our hopes—now dashed—had once been raised as steps. But we refuse, if not with them, to move beyond the brink of signs by being slain, keeping as we do to a path already blazed to lead away from bliss and overstep the abyss of disgrace.

Radical or not as poets among others, but now, I suspect, only unwillingly or all too self-consciously so—are we to even imagine a task for ourselves, or is imagination itself immaterial? Are we keeping in mind the impossibility of being counted among "the poets" as we ourselves, on a margin of sorts, have understood them to be? What is to be done? To have been taken beyond a frame from which one will never escape, one must by definition have become an iconoclast along the way, or one must blaze the way but not come back alone. Having become iconoclasts who are nevertheless bearing messages of a parousia already apparent to only the weariest of eyes, we will, as always, be beside ourselves, tied as we are to the very idols we try to cast-down. What with the furious wherewithal so typical of those who at the end of a given age refuse to set any kind of stage for what is inevitable, and who must therefore far less purposefully take the stage themselves—not just to stay alive, but more importantly, to literally court disgrace or fly accursed in the face of assent: so it appears as well that, if completed or at least counted-down to the beat of even a single heart, enough engaged to yet attain to, but never escape from confrontation with self-consciousness and God, still comes the day that by and large we will have said: *we will be gathered for a martyrdom.*